THE JOYFUL LIFE

The Joyful Life

BY

MARGARET E. SANGSTER

CURIOSMITH

MINNEAPOLIS

Published by Curiosmith.
Minneapolis, Minnesota.
Internet: curiosmith.com.

Previously published by THE AMERICAN TRACT SOCIETY in 1903.

All footnotes have been added by the publisher.

ISBN 9781941281598

CONTENTS

FOREWORD

Each chapter of this book is a simple and friendly talk on some theme of homely interest, and the author's aim has been to suggest something helpful in each as to life and conduct. We are all wayfarers, and our manners on the road have much to do with our happiness and usefulness.

As a rule the pilgrim who walks lightly encumbered with luggage is least weary at the end of the day, and therefore the aim has been to inculcate care for the realities and to let the superfluities go. Most of the impedimenta with which we weight ourselves here will be forgotten when we cross the river and enter the Father's house. Some things we shall carry over—our love to Christ and to each other, our share of the peace that passeth understanding, our desire to do his will and to bear his image—for it is written that in the Jerusalem that is above, "His servants shall serve him."

It is the writer's hope that every word she sends forth may find a lodgment in some sympathetic heart, and that each reader may be her friend. As friends together we may talk of the common experiences which, when love touches them, wear hues of immortality.

MARGARET E. SANGSTER

Chapter 1

THE JOYFUL LIFE

In summer time we hear everywhere in nature the note of joy. Brightness and vividness of color are seen in flower and leaf, forest aisles are sweet with bloom, gardens renewing their beauty, orchards dressed in embroidery and fretwork of blossoms, birds on the wing, and song resounding. The outgoings of the morning and evening rejoice. The winds, soft as zephyrs or tumultuous with sudden tempest, still are attuned to the one exulting chord and Nature lifts up her praise to the Creator whose hand ordains her seasons and guides them in their course.

How is it in that other more intimate realm, where the spiritual life flourishes? Here, too, yet not only now, there should be gladness. The joy of the Lord is your strength, ye who trust in the Lord may declare; the firmament for you is starred with lights that no darkness can dim, and—

> The voice that rolls the stars along
> Speaks all the promises.[1]

In our busy days and hurrying tasks some of us forget that

1 A quote from *The Faithfulness of God in the Promises* by Isaac Watts.

we may be busy and still blessed; toil strenuously, and yet wear singing robes. Christians of a former and more introspective period than ours were wont to talk much of assurance, to long for and prize it, to lament its lack in their consciousness, and to cry out for it earnestly in their hours of prayer. In an age when we are losing the deep sense of the fear of God from individual and family life we hear little about assurance, and there is some danger that Christians are ceasing to cherish what is in truth their very highest privilege and their chief distinction. Assurance of our right to claim kinship with the Elder Brother, a sweet, full, never-ceasing awareness that we belong to the Divine Father, is the inheritance by right of all who are Christ's and who live by faith in the Son of God. No one can have this confidence of acceptance, this security of communion, this feeling of the child at home in the Father's house, and not know often the thrill of an ecstasy surpassing earthly pleasure; the steadfast joy of a soul at peace beyond all perturbation and strife.

We look for a heaven of joy, dear friends, a heaven where there shall be no terror of a parting from our loved ones, no grief, no sin. There the redeemed shall walk in white; there the anthem is forever rising, the harp notes forever ring. Angels and saints, the vast kindreds of the cycles past and to come, the innumerable company of the redeemed, shall dwell there in a bliss that shall never be broken.

> O Paradise, O Paradise,
>   Who doth not crave for rest,
> Who would not seek the happy land
>   Where they that loved are blest,
> Where loyal hearts and true,
>   Stand ever in the light,

All rapture, through and through,
In God's most holy sight?[1]

But we need not wait for heaven till we drop the garments of our flesh. To the disciple heaven may begin, and may continue all the way along, for has not Jesus said, "I am the way," and is there any heaven comparable to abiding with Jesus? What matter a few passing trials, a few rough stones, a few tears and struggles, if we are faring onward with Christ and every step is homeward, and home is spreading its tabernacle over us by night and providing our refreshment by day.

When I met my friend, who had lately heard of the death of a dear daughter in a distant land, a loss unexpected, and leaving her desolate, her look was not cast down, nor was her countenance sad. There was in her expression something chastened, something aloof from the common experience, something elevated, as if she had drawn very close to the home within the veil. A rare illumination from the tranquil acceptance of God's will and the unshaken repose in his goodness which belongs to those who never doubt nor protest nor gird against the arbitrament of the Father, was in her face. "Can I be other than joyful," she said, "in the joy that God gives me when he stoops to take my dearest to himself?"

This joy may be ours, too, in times of illness and languor. I have no sympathy with that cult which denies that illness and languor are possible, which illogically tells us that matter has no existence, and which denies the disciplinary process of pain. Not that our Lord cannot heal, and does not heal, our sicknesses every day. "The healing of his seamless dress is by our beds of pain" always. He is always coming to us when

---

1 A quote from *O Paradise! O Paradise! Who Doth Not Crave for Rest?* by Frederick Faber.

we need him with the gentle command, "Daughter, son, I say unto thee, arise!" But he has many a method for refining and purifying his own, and every good physician, and every adequate remedy, and every hospital room and surgical tool and modern appliance, every ingenuity of skill and science, each and all are his; ours to use as he permits, with gratitude to him that he gives what he gives. So we may bear the little prick and the sharp pang, the fever heat, the racking torment, the exhaustion and the distress, when he sends any of them, with something more than mere passivity, with real joy. And which of us has not known invalids, shut in from the world and ensphered in a grace that the world can no more take away than it can bestow?

The Christian's joy is consistent with very narrow circumstances. I have often heard people exclaim against the hampering of environment. Others can go here or there. Others can give large sums to missions or to charity. Others can have the satisfactions that accrue from wide advantages, from generous living, from contact with the best in art and literature. One would fancy to hear these victims of discontent that there were no museums, no galleries, no libraries; that only the rich could enjoy these treasure stores of intellect and achievement, whereas they are by no means the monopoly of wealth. The poorest, who desire, may enjoy much that has been gathered and catalogued and conserved, and placed under proper care and guardianship for the education of the many, not for the gratification of the few. And nature is as lavish of her displays; her open fields and lofty spaces and acreage of mountain and plain can never be absolutely owned by any one man, however many times a millionaire. Nature gives the poorest a right of way over most of her domains.

When daisies go, shall winter-time,
Silver the simple grass with rime
Autumnal frost enchant the pool,
And make the cart ruts beautiful,
To make this earth our hermitage,
A cheerful and a changeful page,
God's bright and intricate device
Of days and seasons doth suffice.[1]

Ah! friends, it is because we are paupers in heart, a very different thing from being humble in spirit, that we are bankrupt of joy. If some of those who rebel at poverty could penetrate the shams that sometimes are the portion of wealth, their foolish envy would be scattered like a morning mist in the sun.

Says Dr. Matheson pithily, "We think of heaven as needing the photographs of earth to make earthly memory! The Mount of God does not need to be made after the pattern of the human; the human has already been patterned after the Mount of God." Heaven may be our portion beforehand, if our love is there; if our thoughts are there; if our conversation, meaning by the word, the whole conduct of our affairs, is already there. What folly to weigh trifles of wealth or poverty in the scale, as affecting our joy. Our convenience, our comfort, may depend on these, but not that deeper, more enduring thing, our humor and mood, our joy. For is not that Christ's joy? "Who, for the joy that was set before him endured the cross, despising the shame!"[2]

It is seldom the Master's will that we carry no cross. Hidden from the sight of those around us, our cross may be revealed only to the eyes of our Saviour. The hidden cross is

---

1 A quote from *The House Beautiful* by Robert Louis Stevenson.
2 Hebrews 12:2.

often the heaviest. But we too, sharing his cross, may endure it, whether or not the world know our secret, as seeing Him who is to them invisible, and a tide of joy, present as well as prospective, may cover the waste places of our lives.

Yet another phase of this subject appeals to us on the practical side. Young people should never be hindered in the Christian race nor be kept away from the Kingdom by the idea that Christianity means gloom. Undoubtedly there are very good people whose religion never seems to brighten their everyday lives. They give an impression of the shadow on the feast; they behave as if gaiety were a crime. Their homes are not cheerful places, and their piety, though real, is austere. These believers are mistaken if they suppose that they are imitating Christ by their sorrowful demeanor. Our Lord when on earth was the center of a cheerful, curiously interested and eager group of earnest men, and crowds of common folk, with their laughter unchecked, their arguments unhushed, their tasks going on as usual, gathered whenever he appeared. The very children ran to clutch his garments, to take his hand. A man of sorrows and acquainted with grief, he was yet no unwelcome guest at the feast and no bar upon any joy. We do him a great wrong when we frighten the children from him by our crossness or our curtness. Gravity and soberness at appropriate times are not inconsistent with true cheerfulness.

I often wish when I see the young hesitating on the threshold of the Kingdom that they might realize how much they lose by staying away. Not a friend below can offer so much of enduring joy as is freely offered by this Friend with the pierced hands and the head once crowned with thorns. The sweetness of his call will be in your soul, dear child of time, to all eternity. You can never know immortal joy if you do not heed it. "Come unto Me," he says, "and I will give you rest." Yes, Lord Jesus, we will come, and receive in this life, and in the life unending, peace, rest and joy, for at thy right hand there are pleasures for evermore.

I am oft alone, dear Saviour,
    Yet I know not lonely days;
Thou art more than home or kindred
    Unto thee I lift my praise.
And by many a desert fountain
    I can Ebenezer raise.

In the throng, Oh! blessed Saviour
    Oft I seek a place apart,
And I find thee coming to me,
    Shrined and templed in my heart.

Thou canst make a sanctuary
    Wheresoe'er thou sendest me,
And in midst of crowds uncounted
    I can be alone with thee.

Joy of joys to know my Saviour,
    Love of loves to feel him near;
Earth can give no other treasure
    Half so precious, half so dear.

Till I meet my lord in heaven,
    I may have a heaven below;
If with him, I stay contented,
    Joyful, if with him I go.

Chapter 2

MOLDING INFLUENCES

We are all agreed that the early impressions are the most enduring and that lasting shape and trend are often given to human lives while children are yet in infancy. A mother's prayers, a father's faith, the Christian atmosphere of the home, the place the Bible holds in the family, are vital influences in childish training, and preempt the little one for heaven before the evil of the world has had time to occupy the heart's soil. It is the privilege of Christian parents to claim covenant rights for their offspring, and to expect that they will early enter into their birthright as children of God. Alas! too often we are careless and inconsiderate, and undo by our example what we are painstakingly doing by our precept. The influences which are molding our precious sons and daughters are often corrupt, or sordid, or ignoble, because we are contended to live a half-consecrated life, to keep back from God what belongs to him, and to realize only fragmentary blessedness, instead of the rounded whole of peace and joy which the Lord bestows on those who consciously abide in him, and in whom he dwells.

Take, for instance, the common mistake of the mother who frets at her children because she is nervous, irritable and much worn in temper and health. She tells them to speak gently, to be patient, to move quietly, to be forgiving and kind. This is good counsel. But she has worries of one sort or another. Money comes in slowly; perhaps she forecasts the future and fears the rainy day. She is aware of lessened strength, or some malady menaces her comfort. Headaches creep stealthily on her busy days, like foes from an ambush. Before she is aware of it her tones are sharp and her frown is shrewish; she scolds and nags; trifles are exalted into affairs of importance; she punishes in anger; she does not accept excuses or explanations, and the home is a place to flee from. All the preaching that this poor mother can find time for is utterly abortive, ruined by her blundering and sinful practice. She is molding, not gentle, self-controlled and considerate young folk of exquisite manners and unfailing courtesy, but hasty, brusque and easily exasperated people, who will imitate her ways until the wrong habit finally becomes a second nature.

I fancy the dear Lord whose compassions fail not, bending in divine sorrow over such an one, and seeking to restore her soul, to lead her again into the paths of righteousness for his name's sake. And if she will but heed the way of peace is easy to find. If but at each morning's dawning she will turn to him first, make a definite surrender of the day to him, ask him to enter the temple of her body, and to cleanse her soul, so that it may be his fit habitation; if, whenever the impulse to sin comes upon her, she will swiftly and silently pray for help, and refrain from speech until she feels the help given, her whole life will be changed, uplifted and brightened. We get too far from our Lord. We are like children wandering in the bush, going around in circles—the home near with its light and warmth, but we, confused and stumbling, turning from it. Nervous and worried women can nowhere find a complete cure except at the feet of Jesus; but he is ever close at hand, and can relieve them, if they will but call to him, the Healer of the soul.

Do we appreciate at its true worth value of calmness in our life with the children?

> Calm me, my God, and keep me calm.
> Soft resting on thy breast,[1]

should be the mother's unceasing prayer.

Nothing is sadder than to observe an anxious look on a little face, a look of dread and deprecation, where confidence should be the rule. Penitence is not dread. The child that grows up in a home sweet with that piety which exorcises the evil demons of worry and ill-temper will be sorry when he does wrong, and will hasten to confess it and, if need be, will accept the just penalty, and thus take the first step toward true repentance and saving trust in the cleansing blood of the Redeemer. The molding influence of vital trust in Jesus, on the part of parents, cannot but prove of ceaseless and beneficent effect upon the children of the household, who should also be children of the heavenly King.

The Bible has a good deal to say about our walk and conversation. It reminds us of the responsibility we have for our words, especially for our idle words. Now, in one phase of our daily life, we all need the suggestion that we should guard our ordinary talk. Many a time we thoughtlessly comment on the actions of our acquaintances, criticize them, and attribute to them motives of which they may never have dreamed. We do not indulge in anything so gross as slander, and we hold ourselves above malicious gossip, and yet, in a multitude of needless ways, we violate the law of kindness which should be on

---

1 A quote from *Calm Me, My God* by Horatius Bonar.

our lips. Those who listen to us, whether they are young or old, either suffer some diminution of the high ideal which they should associate with the talk of Christians, or have a protest, perhaps unspoken, in their minds, against our faults, or, still worse, fall into the same error themselves. A mother is sitting in a group of friends, her own daughter one of the number. A lady is mentioned as having formed one of the contingent at a summer boardinghouse. "I was disgusted," says the matron, "with Mrs. C. She was constantly maneuvering and managing to secure the best seats for herself and her party when we were driving; she tried to out-shine the rest; her boasting grew very tedious and monotonous." Presently the conversation veers toward another quarter and Mrs. C. is forgotten. But if a young girl sitting by has noted the acerbity of reprehension, the sharp dislike latent in the mother's remarks, she will have imbibed the idea that such comment is permissible among gentlewomen. If, further, in the course of events, after a day or two, she is present when her mother receives the offending Mrs. C. most graciously, as if she were a much-prized friend, the girl will have been propelled down an easy descent into the valley of social insincerity. A false compliment as surely aids in molding a susceptible nature into deceit as does any other bit of mendacity.

These are by way of illustrating the alien and evil influences which may deform character. We may multiply them at pleasure. But, equally potential, and equally within our reach, are those holier, happier influences which elevate, expand and beautify the human soul.

First and most important and within reach of every disciple is the presence in hearts and homes of the Holy Spirit. Some of us speak of the vital spirit of God as if we were dealing with an essence or an abstraction, not as if we were alluding reverently to a person. Asking for the Comforter, as we should, accepting the Spirit by faith, and daily seeking to be filled with him, we shall gain a tremendous amount of power for good over all whom we meet. Not ourselves, feeble, inert, erring, apt to make mistakes, but God himself working in us, speaking through us, should be the lever brought to bear upon a sinful world.

Every Christian is of necessity a missionary. Not always to a remote frontier or to a distant land, not even always to a thronged tenement neighborhood, nor to a factory town where temptations abound, often only to our own kith and kin, our classmates, our friends, our homes, do we carry the blessed gospel message.

When anyone communes constantly with the Saviour, is frequently in prayer, and lives first for the kingdom of heaven, and later for earthly gain and labor, there will be around him an atmosphere of fragrance and peace which will attract those with whom he dwells to the blessed Christ. A Christian lad in a shop, a Christian merchant in the counting room, a Christian woman in society will, if wholly consecrated, draw those in his or her company to Immanuel, and the place of his or her service will be Immanuel's land.

To this blessedness may we not attain, who love our Master, and are fain to set our feet in the footprints he has left us on the road through this place of our pilgrimage, to our unending home?

If we honestly hope to train the coming generation into robust discipleship, we must not neglect to form in them the habit, not merely of Bible reading, but of serious Bible study. There is such a thing as using the Bible as a fetish. They do this who hastily peruse a few verses in the morning or snatch a sleepy glance at a psalm or a text at night, opening the Book anywhere, and reading without thought. One's morning watch, never intermitted in health, should include prayer and regular reading, according to a plan. The child who is taught from the beginning to read the whole Bible will be furnished, when he reaches manhood, with a complete armory of weapons with which to resist the wiles of the devil.

I know mothers who never fail to secure a daily half hour for Bible study with their growing children. I think of a circle of young people who daily gather around a loved sister, and read each day four or five chapters of the Word; who are familiar with its highways and byways through consecutive morning study. Questions are asked, and attention is enlisted, but the half hour is never regarded as a weariness; for, in that home, it is the coronation of the happy day.

Sometimes, dear friends, we discover in our own spiritual lives a strange deadness and formality. We respond to no tender touch in the world's bustle, bidding us come apart and rest awhile. We almost question the genuineness of our conversion. Can branches so leafless and barren belong to the living vine? Yet let us never question the keeping love of the dear Lord, who is able to guard us from stumbling, and to present us in his presence, without blemish with exceeding joy. If we lack the consolation of assurance it is through our lack of faith, and faith is the Master's gift. Let us use the little faith we have and cling not to that, nor to any crutch of our own, but to the promises and to the eternal truth and love of God in Christ. Let us simply go on, doing our duty as best we may, and we shall find soon or late that

> It is better to walk with God in the dark
> Than to walk alone in the light.[1]

In some radiant moment the mists shall drift aside, and we

---

1 A quote from *He Knows* by Mary G. Brainard.

shall behold the clear shining of his face. But even if light be never vouchsafed, and we lack the sweet sense of Christ's nearness and of his approval, we must still endeavor to walk with him.

The world is to be won for Christ by hand-to-hand conflict. Individual faithfulness, individual testimony, individual influence, must carry the conquests of the cross over the globe. The spirit of the disciple must be free from self-seeking, and Christ must reign in those who serve him. Then they cannot but everywhere and always show forth his amazing love and grace.

> When I survey the wondrous cross
> On which the Prince of glory died,
> My richest gain I count but loss
> And pour contempt on all my pride.[1]

One more persuasive and benign influence we may mention, and that is the power of Christian friendship. When we who love Christ meet, why should we be so shy of speaking his praise? In our letters can we not slip in some heart word about the King, or send a poem or a leaflet to be a reminder of his goodness? Contempt on our pride? Yes, but loyalty for and pride in our Beloved, who is the chief among ten thousand, and altogether lovely. Well may we crown him Lord of all—Lord of our homes, our ambitions, our friendships and our whole lives. And

> His name like sweet perfume shall rise
> With every morning sacrifice.
> To him shall endless prayers be made.[2]

---

1 A quote from *When I Survey the Wondrous Cross* by Isaac Watts.
2 A quote from *Jesus Shall Reign Where'er the Sun* by Isaac Watts.

Chapter 3

THE CHRISTIAN WOMAN'S OPPORTUNITY

Woman, in Christian lands and in modern times, has always been influential, and her voice, albeit not lifted in the market place, has been potential in the shaping of opinion and the formation of ideals in the home and in society. But as never before, in the twentieth century woman finds herself dowered with responsibility and listened to with attention; gates once closed swing open for her entrance, and there are few avocations which forbid her approach. Indeed, her only limitations at present are those which belong to the peculiarly delicate though elastic organization which the Creator gave her when he set her apart as the mother of the race. Certain rough work of the soldier and the sailor she may never do. Some of the perilous labors of the builder and the engineer will never fall into her hands. But she is not debarred from any pursuits, except those for which she is evidently physically unfitted and which would manifestly interfere with her guardianship of the home and her care of little children.

It would seem, dear friends, as if the economic changes which have pushed so many women out of the seclusion of the household and into the shop, the counting-room and the several professions, have given Christ's handmaidens very marked advantages in carrying on their work for him. The invention of typewriting alone, and its general introduction into business houses, has brought numbers of young girls into clerical situations—a thousand amanuenses and secretaries for every one of forty years ago—and as they sit at their machines, or take dictation, these girls have a chance, by fidelity, by womanly modesty, by happy unconsciousness of self, to show whether or not they belong to the Lord Jesus. They need not preach, they need not say a word, they need only live as Christ's followers in the midst of their busy days, and the sweet impression of their conduct will not fail of its effect.

Recently I heard a man, not a Christian, speak in terms of profound respect of a young woman who was employed as stenographer by a legal firm. "She bears herself, above anything small or self-seeking; she does more than her duty; no one can help seeing that the little silver cross she wears means that she is a devoted Christian." Every King's Daughter, wearing the beautiful little badge of the order, may thus silently be a witness-bearer in her business life, and many a girl who carries no visible emblem may show in her quiet manner, her thoroughness, gentleness and fineness of character, that she draws strength from above. The business woman may well heed the divine injunction to let the light shine brightly.

> A little candle, Lord, for thee!
>   So let it burn where shadows meet,
> While daily in humility
>   I bend me at thy pierced feet.

The girl behind the counter, the girl in the nurse's uniform, the girl who makes bonnets and dresses, the girl whose place is in the factory, the girl who does housework and helps the home life by her services, each in her place has an opportunity to work for Jesus. Sometimes it will lead her to sweet and tactful speech. Sometimes to a deed of beneficence, occasionally to indignant resentment, if there be profanity or sneers in her presence. Whatever the need, the One whose grace is equal to her day will help the Christian woman to testify for her Lord in the place where he has put her. That place may be obscure, but it is never unimportant, and she will ennoble her life as she is faithful in her daily duties. In God's sight there is neither small nor great, but all work is equally honorable in his accounting. Away back in Old Testament days it was a little captive daughter of Israel in the house of the Syrian general who did the Lord's will, and she has remained an example for women as a type of loyal faithfulness through the long ages.

In society, too, the Christian woman has a splendid opportunity to show her colors. Not all homes of wealth and fashion are anterooms of Vanity Fair. There are thousands of refined and beautiful homes where there is consecration to God and the clear shining of pure religion and undefiled. And yet, along with wealth and luxury, march temptations to sloth, to indifference and to sinful apathy. As once to the cultured Greeks the cross was foolishness, so now, in the eyes of many well-mannered, well-trained Americans, the whole realm of religious thought and principle seems an enchanted ground of mere sentimentality—"incomes from dreamland"[1]—and they look with pity on those whose hopes and aspirations are set upon a better world. The prevalent license of speech, the continual breaking of the Sabbath, the increase of social drinking customs, and the neglect of the Bible and of God's house, the omission of family worship and of grace at the table, too, show that in the polite domain of the wealthier classes Christ's

1 A quote from *After the Burial* by James Russell Lowell.

banner is not honored. There is no mission to poverty or sorrow, to the tenements or the zenanas, which is more necessary or more relentless in its obligation than that mission to the palace and the mansion which invites the Christian woman. If she will but be consistent, go from her chamber in the morning with the sweetness of the Saviour's love upon her lips after her watch with him, refrain from doubtful pleasures, illustrate the beauty of holiness in her walk and conversation, as an "elect lady," she may win others to her Lord, and diffuse around her an atmosphere of piety fragrant as the lilies of peace. Her best opportunities will come to her as constantly she lives in Christ and Christ lives in her.

Take the familiar example of the woman's college, where the daughters of various households are brought together from every State in the Union. Here we find a girl, who represents a home vital with love to Jesus, side by side with another who is charming, graceful, ambitions, yet either altogether opposed to religion, or utterly apathetic to its claims. The girl who is pledged to service, by church membership, or by her heart's allegiance to Jesus, can and does impress her companions so that they cannot continue in indifference. Some of them at least will be forced to look at themselves in the light of the Christian's candle, and to decide whether they will be the world's or the Lord's. Others will, half unconsciously, receive some blessing from the young disciple, and her influence will reach further than she imagines, for the benefit of her college and of those to whom, by-and-by, its graduates will go.

A wonderful missionary opportunity is afforded the Christian woman in our times. She may teach, she may be an evangelist, she may go as a physician, or as the wife of a minister, but she will find on many a dark shore the women and the children waiting to be taught of Christ. Mrs. Howard Taylor, of the China Inland Mission, was speaking at Northfield this last summer of the duty laid upon Christian women to illuminate the gloom of heathendom. She told of the unspeakable wretchedness of China, a wretchedness so fathomless that it is no uncommon thing for little girls of nine and ten years of age to commit suicide to escape from it. Jesus said, "Suffer the little children to come unto me and forbid them not."[1] "If," said Mrs. Taylor, "you in America stand by and take no share in helping missionary effort, you are forbidding the children for whom Christ died to come unto him. By our personal sacrifices, by our gifts, by our prayers, we who love the Lord may, in these marvelous years of the open door, bring the lost into his blessed fold."

Apart from the opportunity of the Christian woman as an individual, there is at present the multiplication of efficient organizations and societies through which she may send her contributions and by which she may help humanity and glorify her Saviour. In the Young Women's Christian Associations which are now found in strong co-operative work in our various cities and towns, in Europe, in Asia, in the islands of the sea, there is a cordon of hearts beating as one, and responsive to orders from on high. She who cannot personally visit factories and shops, or personally touch undergraduates in college, or personally comfort and elevate the struggling masses of discouraged women, may give her name, her contribution and her sympathy to the association nearest her, and work by its means. Settlement work also makes its appeals, and commends Christ to the lowly. The missionary society, the prayer circle, the temperance band, all afford the opportunity of organization to the woman who seeks to be widely helpful.

We must not overlook, because it is so conspicuous, the

1 Matthew 19:14.

ever bright and ever beautiful opportunity of the Christian woman in her home—the mother who has her little ones from the earliest hours, who can lead them to Christ, pre-empting the soil for him before the evil one can sow tares; the wife who may so strongly influence her husband for good, bringing him, if unbelieving, to the Lord she loves; the daughter, the sister, the friend within the gates, each has her vineyard plot to keep and tend.

The mother will most surely win her children to the sweet succession of service which should distinguish the family, from generation to generation—one, another, and another, living for God—by keeping her spiritual life on a high plane. The fire never replenished dies out. The Christian seldom attending the sanctuary, seldom reading the Word, infrequent in prayer, is not in touch with heaven.

When we are tranquilized by communion with God, we shall not easily lose our tempers nor often be overcome by the low mood, nor commit sins which lead others astray. Infelicities of speech and conduct, bringing shame upon the Christian name, are the result of a barren spiritual life, of little prayer and of absence and distance from the Master. The mother, sister, daughter, friend, who shows forth Christ, must abide with Christ.

Not far from thee, my Saviour,
But near thee would I dwell.
Would open wide my door to thee
And all thy goodness tell,
Because I see thee face to face,
And ever know thee well.

Remote from thee is coldness,

And weakness in the strife;
Remote from thee is weariness,
And doubts and fears are rife.
But when I hold thy hand I *have*
The blessed heavenly life.

Are there those who have spent their substance for this world's rewards, are aware that their portion thus far has been disappointment and pain? Are there some who have heard again and again the voice of Jesus calling, calling, yet have not obeyed it, and have refused to come unto him? For women, Christ-loved, Christ-honored, Christ-elevated, there is little excuse, if they turn a deaf ear to his invitations.

Let none of us be despondent because we do not see any great results of our teaching, or our efforts. It is not given to us to always know what we have accomplished. It should be enough for us that Christ knows. Perhaps we are only setting in motion a train of circumstances which shall never stop their beneficence till their last ripples break on the shores of the crystal sea.

Chapter 4

THE VACATION MONTH

August has the preeminent distinction of being the vacation month in the calendar. Not that other months of the summer and the early autumn are not equally serviceable for holiday purposes, but in August there occurs a lull in business, a mid-season pause when people can be laid off without disadvantage. Besides, in the increase of material comforts and luxuries, we have gradually learned that change and recreation are beneficial to health so that city men and their families are more and more going to the country at the time when the former can best be spared from the grind of daily toil.

Whenever the summer recess can be so arranged that the whole household may share its pleasures in common, there is a manifest improvement over the plan of sending the wife and children away, while the bread-winner toils on alone at home. Sometimes, where there are delicate babies to be considered, or invalids to be sent to a breezy, rural atmosphere, the husband must, with the self-denial for which American husbands are conspicuous, give up the society of his family and eat solitary meals, and sleep in a lonely house during most of the hot season. Few men of ordinary means can afford a prolonged vacation; they must be content with a fortnight or, at most, a month. If they have resolved to endure a summer of silence and makeshifts at home, they say nothing about it, and there is seldom so much as a note of complaint even in their letters to the absent ones. The wife hears nothing of the stuffy house, the dinners at restaurants, the sudden illness in the night when there was need of ministration, but the battle was grimly fought out unaided; nothing of the clanging car bells, the blasting of rocks, and the never-hushed roar of the town. Her good man is solicitous that she shall enjoy herself, and that the children shall have their fill of fresh air and fun. He keeps his sufferings in the background.

Wise and far-seeing is the matron who, in her vacation planning, so orders affairs that somebody stays at home with those who cannot get away. A shorter vacation taken by all is better than a longer one from which some toiler is excluded. A great deal of comfort and coolness can be secured in a city home, if the wife or the mother is there to watch the ventilation, and to prepare tempting meals for jaded appetites.

Waiving this phase of the subject, however, there arises another and very practical question for us, and that is, how are we to get the most good from a vacation? What should it do for us, and how should it tell upon the days which are to follow when it has passed away?

To be really worth having, a vacation should be complete. We are a serious, and to some extent an anxious, people. We spend our vitality lavishly in our work.

Once out of harness, we ought for the time to vary the routine and to drop entirely the usual cares. The doctor, for instance, a man whose profession is most exacting, whose sleep is often invaded by a call to the sick-room, whose life is one of great responsibility, should seek a quiet countryside, and release from exertion all the faculties which are usually taxed. If he is fond of fishing, let him go out in his boat and spend hours seeking for a rise, or let him sit on the bank of a stream with his tackle, while the tranquil hours drift away in tranquil sport. Fishing may not attract him, but golf may, or mountain climbing, or sailing, or walking. Let him do anything except prescribe for the sick. The *doctor* should take a vacation, and give the rest of the man a chance for recuperation.

So with the pastor. People are much too ready to ask ministers on a vacation to preach, to conduct impromptu services, to help prayer meetings along by a suggestive address; in short, to continue away from home the line of work in which they are engaged while there. This is very thoughtless on the part of the pleaders, and a minister is not only justified in refusing such services, but fairness to himself and his congregation requires him to refuse. No profession takes more out of mortal man than the service of the sanctuary. It is not limited to the preparation and delivery of sermons; it extends to the life of the parish, to the visiting of the sick, the comforting of the bereaved, the counseling of the perplexed, the adjusting of difficulties, the raising of funds for various projects, and the gratuitous performance of unnumbered public functions. A minister arrives at his annual vacation wearied intellectually, physically and spiritually. He is in a state of mental inertia, and needs nothing so much as absolute rest, and an opportunity to lie fallow for a while. Now is his time to go to church, and sit in a pew and listen; to go to prayer-meeting and slip into a place near the door; to read books which merely entertain, and require small grasp of the thinking powers, and to be freed from every social obligation except that of ordinary politeness. His wife, too, the busiest woman in the congregation, should share his holiday, wholly oblivious of the need to please this or

that critical dame, and relieved of the strain which few ministers' wives escape, of hearing sermons as if they heard them not
in their subconscious feeling of their effect on the audience.

"I have thoroughly enjoyed the Lord's house today," said
a friend, one summer evening. "None of my kin were in the
pulpit." She was the daughter of one minister, the sister of
another, and the wife of a third. Every minister and every minister's wife, in city or in country alike, should guard with jeal-
ous care their privilege of an annual vacation, never foregoing
it on any short-sighted excuse of duty to the people. A rested
man can give his people what a worn-out man has not to give.

In these times of great demands upon teachers, some of
them are making the mistake of devoting entire vacations to
study. A term in a summer school, if limited, may prove stimu-
lating and broadening to a tired teacher, but the better part
of the recess should be devoted, not to study, but to dream-
ing in a hammock, or sleeping in a tent, or getting near to
Nature's heart. Teaching is not easy work. The teacher is giving
her pupils soul stuff as well as information, and when vacation
opens the door to her for summer enjoyment and locks that of
the schoolroom, the vacation should not be clipped off at the
corners, nor invaded in the middle, not turned into a device
for something it was never meant to be.

Having used these professional people by way of illustra-
tion, it may be as well to add that what applies to them is
equally pertinent to every worker in whatever field the work
is found. Some years ago Col. T. W. Higginson wrote a clever
essay under the caption, "Vacations for Saints," especially
pointing to the good women on whose shoulders rests the burden of asylums, hospitals, industrial schools and other phil-
anthropic endeavors. It is no sinecure to serve on a board of
management of a charity or of missions, and the sisterhood

who engage in this particular altruistic labor emphatically earn and need a period of respite. One excellent gentlewoman has in her own case solved the problem of securing adequate relief by now and then stepping out of her place for a year, but most of the elect ladies who work in practical charities are grateful for a summer's margin when they may feel no obligation either to attend meetings or to collect alms.

Here let me not be misunderstood. The Christian disciple can never, with any propriety, abate his or her Christian zeal, nor is there pardonable room for God's people to excuse themselves from his service of love when they are away from home. The preacher should not preach, but he should attend church; and equally, when vacation lures the city church member to a rural parish, that person should keep the Sabbath, and set an example of piety when among strangers. I have heard a country parson of the plain-speaking type openly bewail the injury which the summer element in his neighborhood, an element largely composed of church people from town, did to his young folk. We live in a period of increasing and alarming license, of barriers pushed aside and landmarks removed. Indifference and apathy are as chilling to the growth of Christian graces as are open hostility. No vacation should be taken by a Christian from Bible study, from prayer, and from communion with Christ, and the exercise of these duties and privileges will lead to the sort of Christian living which sets a beautiful and consistent example.

Relaxation is often found in change of pursuit, and the mother who has spent a twelvemonth in cooking dainty dishes may be glad to eat delicate fare which somebody else prepares. The catering for the household, however simple the living may be, becomes monotonous after a while, and a woman enjoys a meal which she has neither ordered nor prepared, coming to it as to a novelty. After a year of mending Tommy's trousers, and letting down Susie's tucks, and making Polly's frocks, and darning the stockings for the whole brood, with their father's thrown in as a make-weight, a lady may find diversion in taking up some beautiful fancy work, fine embroidery on fair white linen, or fleecy knitting, or some other feminine handicraft which is decorative rather than utilitarian.

Whether to spend vacations consecutively in a place one has tried and learned to love, or to go about looking for new points of interest, must be decided by individual taste and by the depth of the pocketbook. People may spend a most satisfactory vacation at home, taking excursions to interesting localities near by, at a small cost. One's own living-rooms, bathing facilities, and the proximity of excellent markets, make this perfectly feasible. But change is wise, if it can be compassed. Home seems always sweeter when one returns to it after an absence than when one stays in it always. From the inexpensive farmhouse, where plain and good fare may be had, to the inn of high prices and many luxuries, there is wide room for choice. Many families in these days transform the home as an integer in the vacation, taking camp equipage and establishing themselves in tents for an interval of simplicity and healthful outdoor life, of "roughing it" in the woods, and of doing without appliances which at home are essential. Or they hire a cottage, furnished or the reverse, and transfer the housekeeping thereto. This is an admirable way to secure a fine vacation for everyone except the mother, whose cares are not much lightened, and whose regime undergoes slight modification.

If we visit friends in vacation, there are two or three very simple rules to be observed. We must go when we are asked and expected, and take leave at the time specified in our invitation. It is customary for invitations in these days to state definitely the time of a guest's coming and going. People who entertain many friends find it desirable to arrange a schedule, so that congenial persons may come together, that servants be not unduly taxed, and that the guest rooms be ready and comfortable. A guest must be pleased and appreciative and contribute pleasure to the common stock, must observe the ways of the house, at times efface herself, and be agreeable to old people and children under the roof of her hostess. To be invited to one's home is the finest of compliments, and to pass a vacation in making delightful visits is to taste the honey brew of affection and loving attention.

The essence of good breeding is in unselfish consideration for others. That will be the most successful vacation in which we have made others happy, in which we have not too anxiously dwelt on our own wishes and needs, and in which we have most earnestly tried to live according to the pattern set us by the Man of Nazareth. Only as we are Christ-like can we be sure of Christ's peace, whether we work or rest.

Chapter 5

NEARNESS TO GOD

On that September day, now a part of the vanished past, when our whole nation, and many other nations uniting with us in sympathy, paid funeral honors to our martyred President, the beautiful hymn of Sarah Flower Adams was sung almost around the globe. Street bands played it, hard-handed laborers and swarthy miners sang it, spoiled children of fashion joined in its lofty strain, the rich and the poor, the learned and the unlearned, moved by a common sentiment, touched by a common emotion, joined in the rhythm of "Nearer, My God, to Thee!" One heard it in the churches, in the homes, in the schools. For the moment it took precedence of "America." It was the national hymn of the republic, the hymn that in the last hours had comforted Mr. McKinley, the hymn that expressed in crystallization, the devotion, the love and longing of millions of aching hearts.

> Nearer, my God, to Thee,
>   Nearer to Thee;
> E'en though it be a cross
>   That raiseth me,
> Still all my song shall be

Nearer, my God, to Thee,
Nearer to Thee!

What is nearness to God? The question is a pertinent one to us as we stand, some of us in life's morning prime, some in its fervid noon, some almost home. May we be conscious in the pressure of daily care, and in our joys and sorrows as they come, that God is near us, and we are near him?

In the experience of friendship between loving hearts in the household, there is nearness, in proportion as there is union, and as sympathy in work and thought strengthens the bond. When we love an earthly friend so dearly that our first impulse is to give him pleasure, our most earnest and urgent desire is to do his will, then to that friend we are near. Estrangement brings remoteness. If there creep in stealthily to the sweetest relation, indifference, apathy, or weariness, the sense of nearness ceases. Equally if there arise hostility, anger, warfare, there is an end of nearness, which implies confidence, intimacy and peace.

Using this as illustrative, we may discern how a soul can drift away from the heavenly Father, becoming so occupied with the world and its pursuits that there will be no wish for God, or engaging in ambitions, which are in antagonism to the Divine purpose and nature, may range itself on the side of Satan. Among the crowds who sang "Nearer, My God, to Thee," in their deep bereavement of heart when our President was taken, were persons of both these types. Perhaps the hymn interposed a wedge between their lower and higher selves; perhaps it gave to some a dawning perception of what it might be to share the Christian's hope, the Christian's faith, the Christian's joy.

Though, like the wanderer
The sun gone down,

> Darkness be over me,
>   My rest a stone,
> Yet in my dreams I'd be
> Nearer, my God, to Thee,
>   Nearer to Thee.

None can be near to God in the subconsciousness of waking or sleeping hours, in whom there does not abide all the while a principle of reverence and a continual trust. The lad who saw angels ascending and descending on the ladder let down from the sky was a sinful being, capable of great meanness, most imperfect, most unworthy, and at the very time of his dream of heaven an exile from home, in flight because of a wrong committed against his brother. But notwithstanding all this, he was a devout believer, and from his youth up he remained so. We cannot read the story of Jacob without observing that at no period of his career was he an alien from God. So God cared for him lovingly as he lay down in the desert, and his sleep was radiant with a vision from the rifted canopy of stars above his head.

We may grow in nearness to God in several ways, but we must be assured that we long for and appreciate the state in which, like Enoch, we walk with him, or we shall stay contentedly on a lower level. Aspiration precedes endeavor. Vision is the precursor of effort. It was said by the Master, of the pure in heart, that they should see God. If any man sees, if any man have eyes, opened to the glory and the beauty, the wisdom and the love of the Father, that man will seek after him. The love of the world and the love of the Father cannot abide together in the same soul. When the dominant motive is to know the will of the Lord and intense determination to serve him, there will be what old-fashioned disciples used to talk about, growth in grace.

Aspiration will not waste itself in mere poetic thought, if it be true. The soul that aspires, prays. The more earnestly and constantly one prays, the closer will be the approach to God. Prayer is not only asking for blessings, it is in itself a blessing and a privilege, and when one truly prays one is aware of uplift, of strength, of courage and of power. Enter into thy closet, and shut thy door, and pray to thy Father, and thy Father, which seeth in secret, shall reward thee openly.

After aspiration what? Naturally in sequence, endeavor. Doing the will of God, doing it in little things, doing it wherever he has placed us. In the shop, in the kitchen, on the highway. Not always is the service one we would choose, but if God choose it for us, we are not reluctant; we try to obey. Often the task is set for us in a lowly place, a place of great obscurity. No matter. If God sent us down in the dark, his candle will light our every step. What does it mean to you or me, that day by day we find opportunities growing out of the soil of humility, like forget-me-nots on the bank of the rippling stream, if not that God is assigning us the daily work, and that in his view every place is honorable in which he uses our hands. What cheer and gladness we find in following the Master, even when the clouds gather thickly and the cross weighs heavily. For, dear friends, when the cross is most a burden, it is also most a lever, lifting us skyward.

The temptation to seclude one's self from the activities and contacts of the world, and to step aside and stay in the cloister has come to many a child of God. But, unless He himself shuts the door and puts a hedge around one, nearness to him is not thus surely found. The devil can penetrate into the cell, and thoughts wander even in the brooding hush of the sanctuary. Rather shall we win our way to him by placing ourselves at his disposal, and discover new surprises of his love by living where we may bring others to know the fullness of the Lord's kindness.

Possibly, for some of us, the path into the presence chamber lies by the milestone marked "Giving." What self-denial is involved in our gifts? Do we cheerfully bestow some regular portion of the income we receive that the Lord's work may prosper? Do we contribute our time, our interest, our influence? They who give liberally to any cause feel a personal enthusiasm for it, which is unknown unless they have something invested. The cause to which we give nothing is not dear, does not belong to us. When we deny ourselves joyfully for Christ, we realize that he is our friend. We say, as never before, "I am my Beloved's, and my Beloved is mine." Often our best way to give is through an established agency which carries on a larger work than the individual can undertake; through the society which disseminates gospel literature, or sends the word of God to those who need it, or starts churches and Sunday schools in frontier settlements, or sends missionaries to far lands across the sea. Where we cannot go our representatives may, if we care enough to furnish the means, and as we worship the Lord in our giving, we grow into such acquaintance with him, that our quiet homes are true Beth-els, houses where God dwells.

> Or, if on joyful wing
>   Cleaving the sky,
> Sun, moon, and stars forgot,
>   Upward I fly.
> Still all my song shall be,
> Nearer, my God, to Thee,
>   Nearer to Thee.[1]

---

1 Three quotes from *Nearer, My God, to Thee* by Sarah Flower Adams.

With its final burst of blissful anticipation the beautiful and familiar hymn carries us up to the gates of the city of gold. Its climax is one of grand, sweeping movement and majesty. From our birth we have had constant occasion to thank God for his unremitting, never-ceasing providential goodness, new every morning, and fresh every evening. If we are ready to drop into a mood of pessimism, a good tonic will be found in recounting our reasons for gratitude. They will always amaze us by their number. The disposition in most of us to exaggerate our difficulties and to linger in the shadow of our discouragements clouds much of our sunshine, and it is well to stop now and then and think over all the bright things. When we are most grateful, then are we nearest to God.

Suppose we pause and take an inventory in this informal talk, of our reasons for happiness. Let us not even glance at those things which may appear depressing. What are our assets in the line of satisfaction? Shall we count health as one of them? The doctor's visits to us have been few and far between in the months that are passed. Our children are vigorous and their school life is seldom interrupted. Our homes are cheery. The circle of bright heads around the lamp has not been lately broken by illness, or by death. We often have good news from our absent ones. The boy in business has the approval of his employer. The girl in high school or at college is diligent and faithful. There is always reason for thanksgiving in being able to work, and in having work to do. Those who are idle wilfully lose half the joy of existence. Those who are idle compulsorily are objects of compassion.

In our personal history, that unwritten history which only God knows wholly, we have reasons daily multiplied for giving him praise, especially for the many, many times when we have been able by his help to vanquish the adversary and to overcome the sin that doth most easily beset us! How often have we felt the strong hand of the unseen Friend, helping us when we were in extremity. For all his mercies shall we not praise and bless his name always, and thus dwell in sweet nearness to him?

> For the love that never fails to us,
>   For the grace that ever guides,
> For the comfort of his leading
>   When the soul in him confides.
> Here we thank and praise the giver
>   Of the good that ever comes
> Daily, like a flowing river,
>   Blessing happy hearts and homes.

I think the Christian who has no sweet experience of living near the Lord, has never risen to the blessedness of privilege to which he has a right. The King will give royally if we will receive, but we ask like paupers. We are willing to take the beggar's crust, when there is a place for us at the table spread for feasting. Oh, friends, let us try more earnestly to do his will; let us more joyfully take from his own hand the children's portion.

Chapter 6

CHRISTMAS HOLLY

With December comes the beautiful consummation of the year. Behind us lie Autumn with her varied splendor of coloring and her rich fruitage, Summer with her pomp of bloom and wealth of golden grain, Spring with her sweetness of blossom and tender atmosphere of hope and love. Before us as December's doors swing wide are days of cold and storm, frost, snow, sleet, wild winds by sea and shore, but there also stretches invitingly a procession of happy mornings and evenings at home, and best of all, December brings us Christmas. Christmas, the world's great festival, gathering to itself, as the months and years go by, the sacred associations which cluster forever around the incarnation, is our gladdest anniversary, because we keep it as Christ's birthday. It does not matter in the least whether December twenty-fifth is, or is not, the precise day on which Mary first held her baby in her arms, while shepherds and wise men worshiped him. On some day in the long history of this earth, the fullness of time came, and God sent into it his only begotten Son, on a mission of redemption. By common consent this day we keep as Christmas has been selected as that anniversary, and all nations are joining in the acclaim which arises in its hallowed dawning to praise Immanuel's name.

Still let us joyfully listen on Christmas Eve, as the midnight hour passes, for the echoes of the angel's song, "Glory to God in the highest, on earth peace, good will to men."[1] Still let us watch with the wise men of old and see the star, "brightest and best of the sons of the morning." Still let us bring to the manger our gifts, gold and frankincense and myrrh. For now, as when Christ came to Bethlehem, he comes to be born again in human hearts, and evermore we may sing:

> Thy home is with the humble, Lord,
> The simple are thy rest;
> Thy lodging is in childlike hearts,
> And there thou mak'st thy nest.[2]

There is special fitness in that observance of Christmas which centralizes the happiness of childhood. To those of us who love children, they constantly reveal surprises of trust and possibilities of rare development. We understand why our Lord set a child in the midst of the disciples and said, "Whosoever shall not receive the Kingdom of God as a little child, he shall not enter therein."[3] Jesus in the Yule-tide days is once more among us as a child. No mere mortal child so pure, so docile, so wonderful as he, yet in very deed a child, subject to his parents, and living beside his fair young mother in her little home in Nazareth. Looking at him, as the Child in the midst of us, we are led to look more carefully and with gentler thoughtfulness at our own children and at the hosts of children outside our own households.

---

1 Luke 2:14.
2 A quote from *Thy Home Is with the Humble, Lord* by Frederick W. Faber.
3 Luke 18:17.

What is our first impulse toward the little ones in the home? Most of us without an instant's hesitation answer that we desire the best for them, the best in education, in training, in companionship, and that we earnestly long to make them as happy as we can. Realizing how brief a period in life childhood must be and how soon our dear boys and girls must be pushed out into life with its trials and conflicts, it is natural and right that we should make the children happy. We do this most effectually when we early impress them with Christ's beauty, when we teach them unselfishness, and lead them in the straight and narrow pathway of love.

When we load the Christmas tree with pretty gifts for John and Jean, and induce them for weeks beforehand to tell us what they want and what they hope to receive, entirely overlooking their part in Christmas giving, we do them a wrong. A one-sided Christmas cannot be joyful, even to a little child. The true Christmas spirit fosters self-denial and bestowal, and the child who makes no small or large sacrifice, that he may send a present to some one outside, or give something to his mother or sister, loses a precious opportunity and is in peril of being morally dwarfed.

Come with me to a social settlement on the East side of the bustling city of New York on Christmas Eve. Upstairs and down children are thronging, for the house belongs to them, and is more a home in their eyes than the tenements where they sleep, and snatch such meals as poverty can give them. Here they are, fair-haired Germans, dark-eyed Hebrews, blue-eyed Danes, oval-faced Italians, the proportion of whatever nationality is uppermost in the locality indicated by the type most numerous among the children. They have no fine clothes, though few of them are in rags, for the tenement mother has her own decent pride, and does her best to send her offspring forth whole, if not clean, from her hands. But how cheerful they are, how beatific is their rapture, how charming is the look of motherhood in the faces of little girls, as they lovingly brood over their new dolls, and how delighted are the boys with skates, balls or sleds! When they sing, their whole hearts are poured out in the hymns, and few hearts in the round world are more intensely joyful.

My point is this, that not only we, who are grown-up, should add to our Christmas felicity by making some asylum, or working-girls' club, or settlement, able to cheer its beneficiaries at Christmas, but that we should bring up our children in the habit of good will. Every little one in a home replete with comfort should early learn that he or she can help to brighten the lot of a child who is less well off, of a child whose little feet are treading stormy pathways. The Sunday-school that foregoes its own annual treat, in order that it may provide one for a school elsewhere, will, on the whole, have a more delightful and satisfactory Christmas than the one which simply absorbs all that the fathers and mothers of the church, and its short-sighted teachers will give it.

Let us broaden out a little more. Christmas to some of us brings great store of useful and beautiful souvenirs, some of them very costly, others inexpensive. To give away what has been given to us is usually regarded as exceedingly ungracious, and there are many friendly tokens, so personal and so exclusively designed for their recipients, that they pass into the realm of sweet happenings and dear memories and belong to our treasured things. But of the lovely, even exquisite cards and leaflets and books which we receive, a large number might well be enjoyed and passed on. To the children in a mission school far across the sea, to the parsonage home on our Western frontier, to the children in a mountain cabin in Tennessee, our superfluities of Christmas gladness and gifts might bring great pleasure. Keep this hint in mind for another year, and let the children know that if they do not abuse or destroy their own gifts, but keep them in measurably good order, they may be sent by and by, when they have outgrown them, to give another lease of delight to other children, perhaps under another sky.

Leaving this phase of Christmas, in this discursive talk, suppose we glance at Christmas ornamentation. Not now is the hour of the frail anemone, of the white lily, of the fragrant rose. Not even the hollyhock, the gentian, the chrysanthemum, or any of the magnificent flowers of the fall, belong of right to Christmas. No, we decorate our homes and churches in December with the strong deep green of the cedar, fir and pine, with the glossy leaf and the shining scarlet berry of the holly, with the beaded whiteness of the mistletoe peeping out from sheltering leaves, with the spoils of the woods and the unfading glory of the evergreen.

Ages ago it was written of the good man, "His leaf also shall not wither, and whatsoever he doeth shall prosper."[1] In the deep dark green of Christmas wreaths and the spicy scent of Christmas garlands, there is the renewal in our minds of this assurance of the ultimate success and prosperity of the man who lives to do God's will. True, to such an one there may come ups and downs, and many strange reverses and vicissitudes. The cedar of Lebanon was not raised in a hothouse. The tree that is strong and tough and fair and full of fadeless leaves on sturdy boughs was nurtured under the stars and sun, rocked by the tempest, powdered by the snow, and tried by the fierceness of the north wind. But as nothing can permanently hurt "the tree God plants," so, if we love God, nothing can harm us, but all things shall work together for our good.

1 Psalm 1:3.

Choosing our Christmas presents is one of the most exciting and on the whole delightsome occupations of the year. Women get much more satisfaction out of this than men, the latter being too busy, as a rule, to give to it the time and thought which it requires. On the other hand, men often have a legitimate occasion for complaint, in the fact that the gifts to them of their wives and daughters are frequently far from individual. A man is given something that fills a felt want in his wife's mind, a piece of furniture, or a picture, or some bric-à-brac which helps to furnish the parlor or dining-room. He amiably accepts it, but it has contributed little to his real pleasure. Both men and women, if they enlist in the campaign of Christmas giving, should select their offerings with discretion, judgment and adaptation to the tastes and needs of the one whom they desire to please.

A merry, merry Christmas
    To all who tread today
The age-long road to Bethlehem
    Where once our Saviour lay—
A little child in swaddling clothes
    While cattle near him lowed;
And in the sky above his head
    The Star of centuries glowed.

A merry, merry Christmas
    To every weary heart
That brings its load of care to One
    Who in our grief has part;
A merry Christmas to the soul
    That lowly bows to him,
Before whose face the seraphim
    Grow in their whiteness dim.

A merry Christmas unto all
  Who open wide the door,
That Jesus Christ may enter in
  And dwell forever more.
Exalted be his wondrous name,
  And glory be his own;
Who conquered sin and death for us,
  And sits upon the throne.

A merry, merry Christmas
  To every little child,
Who clasps the hand of Jesus,
  And loves the undefiled,
And may the light of Christmas
  From heaven's fair palace stream
And all the year be brighter in
  Its radiant living gleam.

"Unto us a child is born, unto us a son is given; and the government shall be upon his shoulder: and his name shall be called Wonderful, Counsellor, the Mighty God, the Everlasting Father, the Prince of Peace."[1]

Dear friends, may the next Christmas bring you and me into closer and sweeter relationship than ever before to Christ our Lord.

---

1 Isaiah 9:6.

Chapter 7

LIFE'S UPS AND DOWNS

If life were a uniform level, broken by no vicissitudes and no disasters, with no strange and baffling problems alternating with its seasons of tranquillity and success, it would be perhaps less trying than it generally is, but also much less interesting. Nothing is more tedious than monotony. Nothing wears on the nerves like a stirless calm. The wildest gusts and storms are more acceptable to the mariner than the inaction which is compulsory when the wind moves not.

I once met an old, old lady, who said that her whole life had been as placid as a summer sea. At long intervals some member of her family had died, but as she had no children the most intimate and deep of afflictions had been spared her, and her husband still survived. Strange to say, I did not feel that she was to be envied. Without pain in this world's economy there is little reaching forward to the heights of joy; without suffering there is seldom intensity of thankfulness; without birth-throes there is little apparent growth in the spiritual realm. Life all a plain road, no hills to climb, no obstacles to surmount, no vicissitudes to endure, is not so desirable on the whole, as life which has its struggles, its sorrows and its losses, preliminary as they come to the final realization of its triumphs, its consolations and its everlasting gains.

The time for sturdy resistance to the difficulties and temptations of the day is usually the period of youth, when one is facing the future, as well as realizing the present, and when the past does not loom large in one's view. The past of youth is very short; the future looks interminable, and the immediate present is strenuous. Middle age often carries the burdens which youth has brought to it, carries them with a steadfast courage, and a serene cheer impossible to youth; and old age is, or should be, the season of tranquillity: the season of resting on the oars and waiting for the end.

> Sunset and evening star
>   And one clear call for me,
> And may there be no moaning of the bar
>   When I put out to sea.[1]

In retrospective hours we sometimes perceive that we made mistakes in our bygone reckonings. We might have avoided some snares and pitfalls had we not rushed along at a breakneck pace. We might have been less impulsive, and made wiser calculations, and taken precautions against disaster. But what is the use of grieving unduly over what is past retrieval? Better far to be "up and doing with a heart for any fate."[2] The past is gone, but the present is ours.

An elderly gentlewoman was talking with me one day about the fortunes and misfortunes of her family. "There was a time," she said, "when my father owned the entire tract of land in which the city of L—— (a thriving Western city)

---

1 A quote from *Crossing the Bar* by Alfred Lord Tennyson.
2 A quote from *A Psalm of Life* by Henry Wadsworth Longfellow.

now stands. Had he held on to it till values rose we would now be enormously wealthy instead of being worn out with poverty, but father did not imagine its possibilities, and exchanged the property for land that proved to be worth very little."

I know of similar instances. They have been very common in this new and rapidly developing country. And almost invariably I have heard heirs of what-might-have-been speak of the vanished riches that had eluded their grasp with the deepest regret. Yet, as we glance around our acquaintances, we do not always find that wealth and luxury have brought the best things in their train. Young men have degenerated, young women have been led into selfishness and frivolity through a too easy life and the possession of too much money. My friend, whose sons and daughters were noble men and women, need not have deplored the fact that they had been reared in a school where the students acquire self-reliance by some bouts with adversity.

If one can but take whatever comes as part of God's plan, and not as the happening of a blind chance, one will be surer of content. A plan of God in every life, and life joyfully lived in accordance with God's plan, is a good formula for true happiness.

Suppose we fancy, in this twilight between times talk, how one may make the best of things in the days of the Valley of Humiliation. You remember that Bunyan's pilgrim went through this place singing quaintly,

> He that is down need fear no fall:
> He that is low, no pride;
> He that is humble ever shall
> Have God to be his guide.

And you remember, too, that in those gentle glades, the Heart's Ease was very apt to flourish? There are worse places on the pilgrimage than this sheltered vale, where one has much occasion to rest in and call on God every hour.

Once, away back in the years that are sweetest to recall, I knew a group of people, mother and daughters, whom our Civil War had despoiled of their all. They lived in two or three rooms, though theirs had been a wide and stately mansion. They did their own work merrily, though a retinue had formerly served them. They were in need of clothing, sometimes in need of fuel, sometimes of food. But I never saw them otherwise than gay of aspect and brightly ready to meet every experience with a smile. It was not resignation they showed, nor fortitude, nor even courage. It was a combination of the three qualities, and the element that fused it was an unfaltering religious faith. One morning an acquaintance and I met in a call at their house. When we came away this lady said severely:

"Well, I call such conduct reprehensible. Those women should have been sewing, making up that bolt of cloth the society sent them last week. Scissors haven't touched it yet! And they were reading, if you please; reading 'Cowper's Task' and Sir Walter Scott's 'Tales of a Grandfather.'"

For my part I had no censure to make. In due time, no doubt, the white muslin was fashioned into useful and needed garments, but the old Southern habit of browsing in a library, of reading over and over the books made dear by the use and wont of a lifetime was more precious than any article a woman's fingers could fabricate. Those ladies were not dependent on new books. Those which they had inherited from book-loving ancestors were sufficient for them, and they had culture as opposed to the swift, superficial intelligence of a later day. Years after I met them, now on the top wave of success.

One girl, was an artist, another an author, another a teacher, and the old mother, still in black silk, with lace ruffles at neck and wrists, continued to read Cowper and Sir Walter Scott in unbroken serenity.

Ups and downs in life are like an undulating land. In America it is peculiarly the case that he or she who is down today may be up again tomorrow. Business reversals and successes are as recurrent as the movement of a see-saw in commercial towns. But the changes of feeling and condition which are consequent upon wealth or its opposite are slight compared with those born of the inner life. Material things are less potential than spiritual. Externals never strike so deeply into the soul as the experiences which spring from the soul itself. The wounded spirit who can bear? When friends prove disappointing or false, when the beloved wander into wrong pathways, when the heart strays from its childhood teachings and loses its first love, when the chill frost of doubt benumbs faith, then one learns what real distress is. When one mournfully says, in the despair of the unmoored and shipwrecked hour, "A believing heart is gone from me,"[1] he touches the bottom of earthly trouble. Yet here, too, there is help for whoever shall seek and accept it from the Word. "He that cometh to God must believe that he is, and that he is the rewarder of them that diligently seek him."[2] When one, climbing from the depths of hopelessness and infidelity, gets a firm footing on that rock, he may ascend at last to the uplands of God, where he shall say, "I know whom I have believed and am persuaded that he is able to keep that which I have committed unto him against that day."[3]

---

1 A quote from *Life's Heaviest Loss* by Frances Brown.
2 Hebrews 11:6.
3 2 Timothy 1:12.

There are temperaments which are naturally sanguine and even mercurial, and they stand their possessors in good stead in many an exigency. Others are easily disturbed, and inordinately depressed by untoward incidents. There are forward folk who are fretful and cross oftener than they are amiable, and moody folk whose persistent despondency acts on their friends as a wet blanket.

One of the most successful recipes for curing the blues, no matter what the source, is to engage actively in some work outside one's self. The tonic of necessary labor is not always within reach of the rich, and so, occasionally, they drift into apathy and from apathy into nervous prostration, troubles which they would escape if compelled to exertion. Of a wretched hypochondriac, a wise physician once said, "She would soon recover if she were obliged to do her family washing." Unselfish work for others is a sovereign remedy for melancholy. Forget yourself. Do good to some one else. As the poet aptly says,

> Is thy cruse of comfort failing?
>   Rise and share it with another,
> And through all the years of famine
>   It shall serve thee and thy brother.[1]

Through the various ups and downs of a very uncertain world, I advise people to cling to a home of their own. No matter how tiny or obscure your house, live by yourself with only your nearest of kin, if you possibly can. It is forlorn work going back and forth over other people's stairs. Some of us keep house, spread the table, buy furniture, choose our street, spend our money, with a view to what our neighbors think and say, instead of with reference to our own means and our

1 A quote from *Is Thy Cruse of Comfort Failing?* by Elizabeth Charles.

honorable independence; in which we are amazingly foolish. Living beyond one's income is a fruitful occasion for downheartedness, and justly so. A little margin, be it ever so little, insures peace of mind and cheerfulness, but he or she who is on the ragged edge of financial incertitude cannot be radiant.

Amid the many ups and downs of earth, is it not as well to remember that here we have no continuing city, but we seek one to come, and so, to keep fast hold upon heaven and God? A life allied to God is stable, come what may.

We are not left to rely upon mere sentiment for this alliance. We have footholds carved in the uphill road. The Saviour has trodden it, the saints have followed him; it leads to the light that streams from the Father's house. The Christian who lives in daily dependence upon God, consciously, lovingly, earnestly calling on him for aid and support and wisdom, must ultimately be victorious.

Thoughtful Bible reading is a great help over hard places. There are so many parallel cases to our own in the wonderful narratives of the Scriptures. So many bits of counsel, adapted to our needs, let that need be what it may. So many songs in the night. So often a feast of manna for the famished, or a fountain of water springing up to quench the thirst of the wayfarer. I wish we who read oftener memorized the clear words of truth, and that children were induced to lay them up as a part of their mental wealth. For in the ups and downs of mortal life God's word is an unfailing cordial, a ceaseless inspiration, and a constant promise of his presence by night and by day.

Chapter 8

A NEW YEAR MEDITATION

One of my old schoolmates, a girl who used to sit at the same desk with me when we were in our teens, came not long ago to make me a little visit. In our different ways we have both been very busy since those bright days when we studied French verbs and Latin conjugations together, and dipped into mathematics and explored ancient history, albeit our school was only a seminary for young ladies, and the era of the woman's college had not yet dawned. In passing, let me say a good word for the fidelity of the old-time preceptors and the thoroughness of the instruction they imparted. I am not disposed to undervalue anything in the latter curriculum, but there were well-educated women, cultured, disciplined, and broadened by their intellectual training, before the great colleges set wide doors open for the entrance of girl-students. After all, the best result of an educational course is seen in its success in putting tools in the hand for use in the life-work, and in the symmetry with which it develops character.

We talked late, Miriam and I, just as we did in our twenties, but much of our conversation was retrospective. So many of those who had been once with us had gone across the river to the blessedness beyond. So many of those who remained were in far lands, or, in the activities of the world, had disappeared from our ken, that we had a new sense of the changefulness and loneliness of this earth.

> I'm a pilgrim, and I'm a stranger,
> I can tarry, I can tarry but a night,[1]

means more to us now than it did in the May morning of our youth.

Miriam is a bright, breezy person whose heart is the gayer because she is the mother of a house full of children, and has always had young people about her, needing her counsel and coming to her for the settlement of her vexed questions. She does not look her real age, but then nobody does that any longer; we are all ten years younger than we used to be, so much more closely do we follow the laws of health, and so much greater is the ease of modern living, what with labor-saving contrivances and luxuries of which our mothers and grandmothers never dreamed.

I remember hearing my mother say that she put on the cap which she wore when she was past seventy on her thirtieth birthday. A matron whom I knew when I was nineteen said soberly, when she was thirty-four, "I am now middle-aged. I must lay aside youthful pomps and vanities." Today, the woman, married or single, who is under forty years is a young woman, and her looks convey no other impression. At fifty the gracious lady bears herself as thirty-five was wont to do two score years ago, and the active person of sixty is far from claiming immunity from service, or any privileges of ease, on account of her age. Miriam and I felicitated ourselves that this is the golden age of the grandmother.

1 A quote from *I'm a Pilgrim and I'm a Stranger* by Mary Dana Shindler.

"But, my dear," said my friend musingly, "how short the years are getting to be. Don't you recall what a long, long space of time a year was when we were children? On a New Year's Day, if we looked forward—and no child ever looks backward—the future was lost in dim and shrouding mists. Now twelve months is a little flitting period, which makes one think of the simile of a bird flying through a lighted hall, from blackness to blackness."

"Well," I answered, "I grant that the seasons do glide faster with one than of old, but I think it is simply because I have so much to do, and so many complex interests. When every day is filled to the brim and the days weave themselves into weeks, the weeks into months, and the months into years, with the rapidity of the unresting loom, what is one to do? Of course, your years and mine slip quickly away. I can fancy, however, those to whom the progress of time is slow enough, even in old age. The man who was once in the midst of affairs, but on whom a creeping paralysis has set its fettering hand; the woman chained to her bed by a cruelly torturing malady; the prisoner in his cell; the stranger lonely among strangers, may not find the years so swift. Part of the restlessness which makes some old people so unhappy is no doubt due to the fact that their empty days have grown slow and dragging, that there is no flavor left for them in life's cup. People in the shadow of grief always suffer from the tedium of the days. The mourner's days move at a snail's pace."

Miriam thought this was true, and for a while we were silent. You may be silent with an intimate friend, and the need to be entertaining of set purpose is nonexistent between those whose mutual understanding is flawless.

After a while she said, "Another year is coming. Are you making any new departures, any new resolves? There is something attractive about turning the fresh page, isn't there?"

"With Susan Coolidge, I have long felt that every day is a fresh beginning, and I have laid aside the habit, if I ever had it, of celebrating the new year as a special place for good resolutions. I do like, though, to signalize it by some particular pleasure, to meet my friends and kinsfolk then, and to exchange greetings and good wishes with them. If the calendar did nothing else, it would remind us that the chances for making our beloved ones happy are lessening, and that we ought to avail ourselves of every coming opportunity to scatter sunshine on the pathway of all we meet."

"But," persisted Miriam, "you would not influence others to pass by a New Year's milestone without some effort to start anew in the Christian race, would you? Suppose you were talking to a crowd of students, is there nothing you could suggest as very apposite to them at such a time?"

"For one thing," I said, "I would counsel all who have never yet done it, to begin on January first a daily definite study of the Bible. There is a good deal of Bible study just now, it is true, but also, in hundreds of Christian homes, and by thousands of young men and women, the Bible is a neglected book. The young people who are familiar with the Scriptures are not too numerous—those I mean who can turn at an instant's call, without hesitation or embarrassment, to any reference text in the prophets, the psalms, or the New Testament. We live in an age of much literary enterprise, when the printing-press scatters new books as the forest trees scatter leaves in the autumn; when newspapers are multitudinous, and every man, woman and child reads something. That many otherwise liberally educated men and women do not know the Scriptures, even as literature, is a misfortune, for they are a treasury of noble words in many incomparable styles. And, by searching them, those who would obtain eternal life still are rewarded by the Divine Author. Yes, I wish I could urge the young people of our land, wherever they are, to begin to read the Bible daily, to read it through in course, or to read it for its poetry, history, and philosophy. I wish they would read it for the life of the Master. On a shelf in my library are many lives of Christ, but none equals, none approaches, the life so simply revealed in the gospels of the four evangelists."

"What besides the Bible," said Miriam, "would you suggest for the reading of a bright, ambitious boy, or of a girl who had her life before her?"

"My preference is strongly for a biography over most other books, but, in a general way, I would tell a young reader to choose what was most inviting, only securing a little regular time every day for some thoughtful reading. Some like essays, many more enjoy stories, and we get the most profit, I think, when our reading is not perfunctory, but is pleasurable and recreative. Libraries abound, and there is no reason why anybody should starve when the table for the mind is so free and so abundantly spread."

This talk of ours was resumed on another occasion when Miriam and I were not alone. A clever young girl was with us, and she had her opinion and expressed it very earnestly.

"I know," she said, "what people of my age need, and that is agreeable companionship. We are restless and dissatisfied unless we are in the midst of things. I would tell every one I knew, especially if she or he happened to be a little blue, as young people often are, to get to work, not merely in wage-earning work, though for many that is a necessity and to some a resource and duty, but to join a Christian Endeavor Society, or an Epworth League, or the King's Daughters, or some brotherhood, or friendly society, and give to it the best one could.

A good time to join the procession of Christian workers is surely the New Year. And, if one is already in, but has been a laggard or unfaithful, may there not be wisdom in reforming, shaking off sloth and beginning over with enthusiasm? I do think young people should assist their pastors more than they do, and what better season for a start than at this very time? Those who have leisure could help him in making calls on the sick or the lonely; others could enter the Sunday-school."

So spoke Caroline, and we older women agreed with her. Only as we give in this world do we get good. I have been reading the life of a great missionary, Verbeck of Japan, and it has been borne into my soul that the only life worth living is the life of Christian love. It may be spent, as the foreign missionary's is, under a distant sky, as the home missionary's and colporter's, in the waste places of our own great land, as the minister's in his parish, as the mother's in her household, but if it be a life after the fair Christ-pattern, it will be a life poured out for others, and therefore very blessed.

Friends, I think we stand in the portal of another year. God gives us more days, more weeks, how many or how few we know not, but they are sent straight from heaven, and we are to use them for him. Have we made mistakes? It is not too late to rectify them. Have we committed sin? We may find cleansing in the fountain where all uncleanliness is washed away. Have we been discouraged? "As thy days, thy strength shall be,"[1] is the word of the Lord to our weariness and faintness. As we wait, not knowing what shall be on the morrow, we may fill the measure of today with contentment, surrender and sweetness. And from the sky the everlasting Father, speaking to our need, says, "Certainly I will be with thee!"[2]

1 Deuteronomy 33:25.
2 Exodus 3:12.

This meditation grows too long. But I have one more practical suggestion, and that concerns the storing of the memory, as a hive with honey, with worth-while things to have and to hold. You would find it much to your profit, dear reader, to study by heart at least one verse of Scripture every day in the year, to learn a few noble hymns, and to fix in your minds some fine strong thoughts of great writers. Memory may be a good servant, if trained, not only in early, but in later days.

Chapter 9

INCOMPATIBILITY

Among the greatest of our smaller trials, if the paradox may be pardoned, must be reckoned incompatibility. To live in daily contact with some one whose ideas are in jarring contrast with your own, to endure the moods and tempers of a person who rasps you by voice and emphasis to the point of a continual irritation, is to wear the medieval hair-shirt, and endure the medieval scourge. A sweet-faced serene saint of God, whose way in life lies through the drudgery of a New England kitchen, once confided to me, in a moment of supreme disheartenment, that there were times when she longed for the rest of the grave, smiling, as she added, "I am perfectly worn out by the companionship of Aunt Tabitha; yet she is the salt of the earth." Good people may be intensely uncomfortable neighbors, and an excellent woman prove herself as wearing to her family as a mustard plaster next the skin, burning, blistering and unbearable even by the help of patience. There are kind souls in this world who defeat their own impulses by performing unselfish actions in a tactless and disagreeable fashion, which cannot but provoke antagonism; and there are persons admirable in their integrity and their regard for principle, who, nevertheless, are instruments of unceasing discipline to their families. As a rule such people are calmly oblivious to their personal defects, and tranquilly ready to throw the blame of whatever misery follows in their wake on the shoulders of others. *They* are never in the wrong. Their ill-temper is, in their own eyes, righteous indignation, and their contrariness, devotion to propriety; yet the sum of much household cheerfulness is sadly lowered because of the absence from the home of the element of congeniality, and the necessity therein of continual repression, self-denial and forbearance on one side.

I am led to this special line of thought by the dilemma of a young couple who find it their duty to admit to their new home a relative whose claim upon them is two-fold: she is too feeble to support herself, and, in a wide circle of kindred, nobody else will have her. The nephew who feels called upon to give her the shelter of his roof is quite aware that her presence will be a trial to his wife, yet he sees no other way in the matter, for Great-Aunt Nancy is old, dependent and fretful, and she absolutely refuses to be supported among strangers.

The bride naturally regrets that in her new home, which she had hoped to make a bit of Eden, there is to be an inmate whose all-pervading influence will rob it of much of its charm. But she is bravely making up her mind to the inevitable. She has set aside a sunny chamber for the old lady, and has resolved to make the best of things, since Jack is sure that there is no other course to be taken.

The man of the house, going to business daily, escapes much of the unpleasant friction which is the accompaniment of his wife's life, when an uncongenial person is with her from dawn to bedtime. If, however, she sees the thing clearly, and accepts it bravely, half the battle is won. A nettle grasped firmly in the hand does not prick and wound as much as one that is carelessly encountered.

I have little credence to give to the theory that hateful old people are the product of untoward circumstances. Frowardness of temper probably began in the days of youth, and an uncurbed unchecked selfishness years ago indulged and fostered, is at the root of the elderly perversity. One meets sweet old people every day, people who have mellowed and ripened under the storms of life, and who have gained beauty of soul and face as they have borne privation, anxiety and suffering. Nothing from without ever makes man or woman peaceful, or the opposite. It is the heart life that tells on the behavior. When a young woman is fretful, unreasonable and capricious, when she sees only her own point of view, and is disposed to consider herself before others in the little as in the large occasions of home life, she is surely stepping forward on that road which leads straight to a meddlesome, interfering and dreaded old age.

When it can be managed, young people should strain every nerve to begin their united lives without the presence of any third person. They are far better by themselves, especially in the early years when more or less adjustment must be taking place. To their future, their present is ministering, and if no one is near to comment on their mistakes, or to take sides if they happen to disagree, their chances of harmony are increased. Still it is now and then a plain duty to widen the home and take into its sanctuary another inmate who may and may not be an addition to the home's stock of peace.

A lady, who was to her fingertips a gentlewoman, delicate, dainty, and accustomed to a quiet elegance of routine in her housekeeping, some time ago found it her clearly indicated obligation to admit beneath her roof a group of young people whose home had been swept away by a flood. Into her fair domain they trooped like the vandals who invaded Rome.

They were boisterous as a March wind, untrained in refinement, and utterly ungracious and unthankful, but they had to be endured for a while. The trial was no slight one, though, as the lady said, it was not to be mentioned in the same day with incurable disease, or a fire, or a death in the family.

Our way of bearing such attacks upon our equanimity shows of what stuff we are made. It reveals our philosophy or our lack of it; yes, we may go a step further and say that it shows our Christian character, or our imperfect faith. If it be God's will that we are to dwell with those who seem to us incompatible with our peace, God can give us grace for this as for any other trial.

We may take to our souls this great comfort: that we never have to make provision for the whole journey, but merely for one step at a time. The miracle of the daily manna is ever repeated in the commonplace lives of modern Christians. Forecasting a weary monotonous stretch of the road, we wonder how we are ever to accomplish the distance between the milestones. But the Lord has never bidden us to worry and waste our strength in this effort. He has simply ordered us to go forward, and has said that he will give us grace in time of need. "If thy presence go not with us, carry us not up hence,"[1] we may pray, awaiting the answer that will come ringing from the skies: "Certainly, I will be with thee."[2]

People who are bad company for others are bad company for themselves. Once in a while is it not a good plan to be very faithful in our self-examination? Are we guiltless in our Lord's sight so far as our intercourse with others is concerned? Are we gentle, tolerant, cheerful, amiable and self-controlled? In some rooms there hangs upon the wall an illuminated card bearing

1 Exodus 33:15.
2 Exodus 3:12.

this legend: "Christ is the head of this house; the invisible guest at every meal; the unseen listener to every conversation." We may not suspend this card from a peg in the chamber or the dining-room, but the sentiment, the thought, should be ever with us. And if, indeed, Christ Jesus is with us, and we live as in his immediate sight, we shall not often be cross with children, impatient with young people, exacting with servants, or unfaithful in the performance of our tasks.

The really brave soul does not waste time in thinking very much about itself, and is far from wasting its strength in self-pity for imaginary wounds and bruises.

In the least lovable nature there is something to love, if it can only be found. Human beings are very complex, and nobody is repellent all through and to all advances. A little child may find the key that unlocks the sealed tenderness in an aged heart. If you can use but the right *sesame*, you may open the most closely barred door. A woman known to me was the dread of three generations for her coldness, moroseness and general dissatisfaction with her little world and with the kith and kin whom she affected to despise. But in her later life there was thrown upon her the care of a helpless family of mother-less children, and she amazed all who knew her by fidelity, kindness and self-forgetfulness in the new role.

By living as in the presence of Christ we shall gather strength for any emergency, and be armed against needless suffering and sorrow. Like Brother Lawrence, that humble monk of a by-gone century, like Santa Teresa, like Elizabeth of Hungary, like John and Paul, and "the elect lady," and like thousands unnamed and unchronicled who have, through faith, subdued kingdoms and wrought righteousness, let us live always, find-ing our Lord in every hour and in every action. For nothing comes by chance. Our lives are a plan of God. If to any of us smooth things are not appointed, it is because God sees that we need rough things. By whatever wind God sends, the Christian's boat is sailing to the port of Peace.

A man that hath friends must show himself friendly. In the chill days of March there are blasts as rigorous as ever blew from the frozen north; but there are moods of sunshine too, and sweet breezes that coax the early flowers into bloom, and allure the bluebirds from the thicket, and give the land a first pledge of a coming April and May. Friendliness is like the sunbeam that thaws the icicle. The most unsympathetic temperament melts before the magic of persistent kindness.

If any of us is carrying the sort of burden which God has given us, and which is the heavier because it has to do with the closeness of earthly relations and the intimacies of the fireside, let him not try to cast it off, but rather remember the injunction, "Bear ye one another's burdens, and *so* fulfil the law of Christ."[1]

The great Duke of Marlborough had a wife whom he adored, but who was a beautiful termagant. He bore her caprices, her furies, her frequent gusts of unreason, with a gentleness which was remarkable in one who was accustomed to receive deference and to be obeyed when he commanded. One day, that she might vex her husband, the Duchess cut off her beautiful hair, which he was accustomed to caress, and left it lying where his eyes must fall upon it. But her intention missed its aim. To the day of his death this man of iron self-control never referred to the incident, never reproached her, never seemed to see what she had done. The shorn tresses grew to their former length without a word from him. But after his death, among his precious things in a cabinet under lock and key, those who survived him found the glory of her hair

1 Galatians 6:2.

as he had gathered it up and laid it away. Incompatibility of temperament had not been enough to make discord in a union where one was invincibly patient and unconquerably loving.

One generation passeth away, and another generation cometh. Each respects the errors of the preceding, and each may derive profit from the successes of the preceding. In the peace that passeth understanding, no matter what the outside perturbations, we may all be kept if we but ask for guidance and trust in God.

Chapter 10

AFTER-EASTER MUSINGS

Easter is the coronation of the Christian year. As we mount the golden stairway of love and faith which leads us to the contemplation of our Lord's resurrection, we realize our right to be called the children of God. As Christ laid down his life to take it again, so we, falling asleep in him, shall awaken to newness of life. To death every believer may smile a welcome, for death but opens for us the door into the house of the Father, where is fullness of joy, and we go no more out forever.

I wonder whether we, as Christians, appreciate the comforts that Easter Day brings to us, or care, as we should, for its promise and its pledge of the eternity which is to be "conjubilant with song." Surely in the deep meaning of Easter there should be for us an abiding peace. We should learn a nobler trust. Our attitude toward the next life should be more confidant, less shrinking, more serene, and when our loved ones go we should follow them with some mingling of gladness in their felicity to sweeten the loneliness of their absence.

One day a woman, whose whole life was a beatitude, sat at her desk, happy in her work, till four o'clock on a Saturday afternoon. At the same hour the next day she was not very well, and that night she slept and drifted into a state of unconsciousness from which she did not waken here. When she awoke she was with God. Her spirit had heard the royal summons, "Daughter, come home," and from the earthly hearth she loved she went, without pain, without weariness or weakness, straight to the blissful abode above. There must have been a glad surprise for that redeemed one when she found herself in the heavenly mansions. People pray to be delivered from sudden death, as if any experience could be more ecstatic for the Christian than just that swift transition from one state of being to another. Nothing but joy for one who thus goes home, though there must be shock to those who remain behind.

Not of death do we think at Easter so much as of fullness of life. All winter we have had bare branches and silent woods, gardens stripped, fields brown and sere. But the time of the singing of birds has come. The orchards are soon to be gay with blossoms. Nature, apparently languid and idle during the period of storm and cold, has been steadily at work in her potential way for months, and soon the world will be waving and fragrant with summer again. In the eagerness of healthful childhood, who does not participate in these happy hours; who is not aware of a thrill of rapture as he listens to the song of the robins, or smells the bloom of the lilacs? Spring has a charm to restore lost childhood and make the old young once more. Every springtide witnesses this miracle wrought anew in you and me.

By the door of an old farmhouse in Connecticut there grows a white lilac bush, lifting its perfumed plumes in the spring air, sturdy and strong whatever winds may blow. The people who planted it went to heaven many a long year ago, and the gray-haired couple who occupied the house when last I saw it are safe amid the fadeless gardens of Jerusalem that is above. Strangers are there now, and the little flaxen-haired brood of an alien race play around the old threshold. But the same flowers come back year by year, preaching the same sweet sermon of the changeless faithfulness of our God. When the last echo of the Easter music has melted away into space, when the Easter garlands are withered, and from the mount of our Easter exaltation we descend to the valleys and the common-places of our daily lives, let this be our ceaseless joy: that God is ever with us. Always the same gospel! He who, year in and year out, sends the shower and the sunbeam, dresses highway and byway with beauty, from the dogwood to the golden-rod, from the green leaf to the brown, will not forget the least of us. His goodness is ever new; his kindness always outpoured, his tenderness greater than our uttermost demand, and the same spring time over and over is sent by the same dear Lord and Father.

In the old days of the Bible there were those who dwelt with Jehovah as we seldom do in our hurrying modern life. Abraham was "the friend of God," and Enoch habitually "walked with God," and we too, in our railway trains and at our work, may have glimpses of the unseen, may walk with God, if we seek him amid the details of our avocation and take time to look upward. What a different world this might be for some of us if we were ever alert to hear the voice of God; if amid the perturbations and disturbances of our days we walked in such sympathy with him that our souls would be tranquil, whatever came to us.

Calm me, my God, and keep me calm,
Soft resting on thy breast,[1]

---

1 A quote from *Calm Me, My God* by Horatius Bonar.

should be the prayer of every one who walks with God.

All sorts of human experiences militate in our time with the contemplative spirit which dwells apart and muses of heavenly things. Many a Christian has a hard time to get along because of limited means. Children to be fed, clothed, and educated; fuel to buy, rent to pay, something to be provided for the future; it takes the whole of man's time and strength, or woman's faith and hope to carry the burdens of responsibility and ordinary work. If religion is good for anything, it is good for sustaining the heavy-laden. Not on Sundays only, with their blessed intervals of peace, but on every week day the thought of God should bring a breath of balm, the presence of Christ should make of the plainest loaf and the scantiest cup a feast. Surely it is not only of the Sabbath that looking back we may say, "He brought me into his banqueting-house and his banner over me was love."[1]

Among the after-Easter suggestions which we cannot forego is one that has to do with the mourning of Christians. When from a household devoted to this world and its pleasures and ambitions one member goes, there may well be gloom that is unrelieved, for where is there room for hope of reunion? But if the child, the husband, the loved one, is taken to *Christ*, the Christian has the sure expectation that in a little while there will be a blithe meeting to compensate for the sad parting. Not perhaps for a longer time than often intervenes in this world, are we divided from those who pass onward, since we never know how soon the summons home may come for us. That other life that seems so distant, may be near, and always

> It's coming, coming nearer,
> That lovely land unseen,

---

1 Song of Solomon 2:4.

It's shores are growing clearer,
Though mists lie dark between.[1]

Habitually to think on heaven as the land of the living, and of our dead as occupied there in loving service, should help us to bear our present bereavements with cheerfulness that conquers grief and makes resignation dignified and tranquil.

Lent, formerly observed only by certain sects in the church, is gradually so winning the hearts of Christians of every name, that many quietly keep it as a period when they may draw nearer to their Master than in the ordinary activities of time. A season of retirement now and then is worth while for any one's seeking who wishes to grow in grace. The forty-days' fast, though only partial as regards self-denial in food and drink, may be profitably kept by abstaining from some of the ordinary social diversions, and by giving larger time than usual to prayer and scripture reading. Would we know the mind of God, let us search the Scriptures which are able to make us wise unto salvation.

"My friend," said a good woman meeting another on the street, "I want you to have a richer benediction from above than you ever have had." The salutation was uncommon. The one who gave it had been herself uplifted by a season of communion with the Most High, it being her custom now and then to spend a day in her closet, giving the hours to prayer from morn till eve.

One day or forty days, let us who have shared the Easter gladness give from time to time a special interval which shall be consecrated to special thought, prayer and study.

Every Christian Sabbath is a commemoration of the resurrection. Every time the bells call us to church they call us to

1 A quote from *Coming Nearer* by Margaret Sangster.

worship the living Christ, the Lord who was not chained of death but in triumph broke its bonds. Entering the sanctuary we show that we are followers of the risen one.

The apostles so near the time when the Lord was crucified, and so happy in their personal knowledge of him before he ascended into heaven, continually preached the resurrection. The New Testament is full of the melody of their triumphant faith. We, nearer to the day of his ultimate triumph over men than they, should have an equally regnant faith. Our daily life and conversation should be set to the lofty chorals of victory, and every Sabbath should bring to us an added sense of joy, a farther-reaching glimpse into the unseen.

How white are the flowers of Easter, lily, azalea, heather, rose; how stainless are the blossoms, we choose for our churches, our homes, and our festivals at this flood-tide of the spring. I remember an after-Easter wedding in a stately church; the flowers, the bride's dress, the white ribbons, all typical of spotless purity. We have such associations, all of us, and though we admit gorgeousness of color, yet the white tone predominates in our Easter adornings. The suggestion is of robes washed white, of sins removed and blotted out, of the garments the redeemed shall wear in Paradise.

> When the Easter chorals cease,
>   When the Easter flowers fade;
> Keep us still in perfect peace
>   In the sunbeam, in the shade:
> Grant us, Lord, the Easter love,
>   Give us, Lord, the Easter hope,
> Till we reach the realm above,
>   And the crystal portals ope.

Not more knowledge, but more love, more child-like simplicity, more spontaneity in our service, are the great necessities of the Christian life today. Is Christ real to you, dear friend? Do you feel that you love him so that life lacking him would be strangely shorn of the beauty, of interest, and of enthusiasm? Do you say in the hush of the twilight, in the heat of the noon, when the great moon hangs golden on the horizon, or the morning tints the east, "My beloved is mine, and I am his,"[1] "I am my beloved's, and my beloved is mine."[2] If so, you may carry with you everywhere and always a continual Easter in your heart and life.

---

1 Song of Solomon 2:16.
2 Song of Solomon 6:3.

Chapter 11

WHEN MOTHER IS BLUE

When mother is blue, I just put on my hat and run away. It takes all the sunshine out of the house, and I can't stand it."

The speaker was a girl of twenty, with an apple-blossom face and merry eyes. One saw at a glance that her life had been free from the pressure of much care, just as one read between the lines, in looking at her mother's calm countenance, that the elder woman had fought a long battle with adversities of various kinds. In that faded face the eyes may once have been merry, but they had grown thoughtful, and it was hard to believe that the matron had ever been reproved in her youth for indiscreet and immoderate hilarity. Yet, as she smiled at her daughter's impulsive speech, she said,

"I was once as gay as Gertrude ever is. In fact, I was noted for my irrepressible spirits. The discipline of experience has toned me down, but I am almost always cheerful."

"Yes, indeed," said the daughter, patting her mother's cheek, "and that is why I am so disturbed when she is out of sorts, the dear brave lady. I feel as if the bottom has dropped out of our scheme of living when mother gives up and folds her hands in melancholy."

I went on my way with a new appreciation of the mother's value to a home. Motherhood implies so much, must mean so much in every environment, and in our households what do we not expect from her who is at the helm? She manages the domestic economy, often doing most if not all of the work with her own hands. She buys the material for the children's clothing, cuts it out and makes it. The weekly mending and darning for an ordinary family is a large and onerous task, and in a majority of instances the mother undertakes and carries it on without assistance. When a maid is kept, or where there are several servants, the routine still demands the continual supervision of the lady of the house, an old-fashioned term which I like for its suggestiveness and descriptive character. It is she who plans and projects, who caters and provides against usual or unusual needs, who frequently makes the finer desserts, and on whom the comfort of her circle depends.

Mother is the confidante of the children, who bring to her their little daily troubles and trials, tell her of their school difficulties and ask her help at evening when they study the lessons for the next day. As her sons and daughters grow up, they more than ever need her counsel and support; more than ever lay their burdens at her feet, and receive from her wise and tender hands maxims and bits of advice as indispensable as daily bread.

A father may throughout the years of their opening lives show indifference, aversion or positive hostility to religion, yet if his children have a pious and praying mother, she may draw them one by one into the kingdom. A Christian mother, one who lives close to God, is almost invincible against the darts of Satan, and opposes an armor of proof that throws off his poisoned arrows and acts as a shield for her loved ones. God has ordained that mothers shall be influential beyond others.

They have the first chance. The impressions they make are the most enduring. I would not underrate nor diminish the potency of Christian fatherhood; but men are less with their families in the home, and less able to lay line upon line and precept upon precept in their children's training, than are women. No Christian mother should ever despair of the ultimate safety, the conversion, and the sanctification of those whom as little ones she brought to the Lord in continual, reverent and humble faith.

But, with everything they have to do, mothers sometimes grow weary. Health fails, trials thicken, anxieties crush. The most elastic nature is not strong enough to cope with never-ceasing financial stress. Just a little more money in many an instance would so ease the machinery of the home, so lessen the load, so brighten the life, that the mother would live longer, be less irritable, be freed from nervousness, and do her best as she is never able to do, handicapped by limited means. Mother is "blue," because mother is worn out. Mother is "blue" because the rose-light of hope has turned to dull gray ash and withered brown in her pathway. The happy young things about her, effervescing with vivacity, overflowing with energy, do not comprehend mother's despondency for two reasons: one is that they are so well and so strong that they have not yet learned sympathy with ill health and feebleness, and the other that they are often in the dark as to the causes of maternal solicitude. With a mistaken kindness parents often keep their trials to themselves and refuse to let young people share them. The life of the home goes on with "a flowing sail," nobody is warned of reefs and shoals, and not until a crash comes are any of the family except the overwrought parents aware that there were danger signals which ought to have been heeded. "I don't want to spoil young lives," says the mother.

In family life reciprocity should rule. With a weakness that has its root in purity and unselfishness parents overbrood their children long after the latter have outgrown the necessity. For example, a man was struggling in deep waters in a period of life when his first strength was spent, middle age with its encroachments had arrived, and pecuniarily he had all to do that he could possibly attempt, in order to save his credit and keep himself from bankruptcy. His situation was known to a friend, who met him one day accompanied by a young and very beautiful girl, his eldest daughter. She was urgently pleading for the money to buy an expensive outfit for a summer jaunt, and she continued her petitions, half in banter, made as a cover for a very evident sober seriousness of intention and desire. The father's predicament was that of an indulgent man who had never denied his child a request that it was in his power to grant. He tried to say No, but yielded in the end, gave the daughter her way, and plunged himself into more tangled difficulties. "I never saw anything so cruel as that young girl's behavior," was the friend's comment; "nor so inane as that of her father. He seemed to me pitiably weak and foolish."

In such a situation, complete confidence would do much to render impossible so unhappy an incident. Parents ought to let sons and daughters know the family resources, and to some extent, at least by self-denial, allow them to share the family burdens. Mother would seldom be "blue" if she were not unduly weighted with the heft of loads too great for her to bear.

But when she is depressed, is it quite fair to run away and leave her to "dree her weird alone"?[1] Sometimes this is what she needs, quiet, seclusion, no one, above all, to jar on her mood

1 Dree her wierd alone—to endure one's destiny alone. (Scottish)

by untimely cheer, no one to antagonize her by reproaches. Often she does want and would respond to tenderness, to gentleness and loving caresses and speech. If she can be persuaded to get out of herself by any tactful ministries, her fit of the blues will soon pass away.

Mothers are very apt to lack variety in their lives. The younger people have the vacations, mothers stay at home and cook and sew. There is a limit to woman's power of endurance. Over many a lowly mound, bedewed by sorrowful mourners with honest tears, might be written, "Died of monotony." Change of scene is better than medicine for many a malady of body and mind. Once in a while a surprise might be carried out by which the youth of a tired woman should be renewed.

I recall a wedding I once attended, where the bride went from her father's house a slender lily-white girl, who had been brought up most delicately in an atmosphere of ease and luxury. She accompanied the husband of her choice into a rough, hard pioneer life in a new State, and there, far from neighbors, from church privileges, or any social advantages, she spent many years. Children came rapidly. Her cares were numerous. She grew old and hard-handed and prematurely bent. At last there was received a pressing invitation from her girlhood's home for her return there, to make a long and restful visit. True to her habit of self-abnegation, she was reluctant to consent, and desired to send a representative in her graceful Maud, the image of herself at seventeen, or her dimpled Agnes, a lovely child of fourteen. But the children were firm. Mother must go, they said, and go she did. A new black silk gown for occasions was an unheard of extravagance, but it was procured; her wardrobe, though very simple, was augmented until she felt that it was presentable, and a shy, reserved, timid stranger, the woman who had forgotten the lightsomeness of her youth, appeared again in her olden place. At first she described her sensations by the homely comparison of a cat in a strange garret; but the unfamiliarity wore off, the rough hands smoothed, and she found that leisure had attractions of its own. People did not know her when she emerged from the enfolding solitude of her far off home, but bit by bit they discovered her to be the same that she used to be, and when, after three swift months had gone, she said that she must turn her face again to husband and children, it was predicted that they would hardly know her there. Nor was it quite the same mother who went home; it was a mother rested, refreshed, and wonderfully rejuvenated; freed from the fettering grooves, and with new strength, new interest, and new delight in living. Such a new lease might be given to many a tired out mother.

In every age, in every clime, the tendrils of the heart cling to the mother. Alike in the far East as in the newer West, she takes precedence of others, with a singular and compelling charm that has its origin in human nature. The one who nursed us in infancy must be dearest and nearest in one exquisite and intimate relation until the end of her life. Mother love is sacred, is unexacting, is glorious. Though poets and painters prefer to dwell on the love of the young mother, holding in her arms the little child, in real life the mother grown old is just as beautiful and as fondly cherished as her youthful sister. King Solomon rose and seated his aged mother beside him on the throne when she entered his royal presence, type in this of every loyal son who does honor to a venerable mother.

The mother to whom we pay no homage is the one, rarely seen, whom Dickens drew under the name of Mrs. Skewton. Artificial, aping juvenility, heartless, fastening her poor old hands in a frantic clutch on the fringes of fashion, her very existence a thing of shreds and patches, one can scarcely tolerate such a travesty of motherhood. One hopes it is a caricature; and yet to this degradation a woman may come in old age, if she live for this world only.

> She has chosen the world and its
> Misnamed pleasure,
> She has chosen the world before
> Heaven's own treasure.[1]

When mother is blue, or a little difficult, or set too much in her own way quite to suit the headstrong wilfulness of the juniors, bear with her and set about bringing back her sunshine. Half the everyday sorrow of this earth would melt into thin air if we were all more anxious to give joy than to get it, to be rather love-worthy than grasping, and to make others happy whether or not we were happy ourselves.

---

1 A quote from *She Has Chosen the World* by Robert Murray M'Cheyne.

Chapter 12

REVERENCE

Writing from his country home to a friend in town, Dr. Oliver Wendell Holmes, then past his three score years and ten, said that on the preceding Sabbath he had attended the Baptist church in the village, adding, "There is a little plant called Reverence, in a corner of my soul's garden, which I like to have watered about once a week."

The old-fashioned virtue of reverence, as it applies to our daily life, is rather deprecated in our modern society. Shakespeare says, "Yet Reverence, that angel of the world, doth make distinction of place 'twixt high and low." It is our boast now, however our observation challenges its truth, that we have no distinctions of rank and class in America; that all men are born free and equal, and that they so remain. Certainly a vast change has come to pass since the New England parson, stately in his ruffled shirt and gold-headed cane, walked the streets of the sequestered hamlet or the growing city, regarded, for the sake of his office and his personality, with veneration by young and old. In Hawthorne's picturesque delineations of Puritan life we find gentlewomen sumptuously arrayed in velvet and lace, while matrons of lesser station were limited to stuff of inferior value and smaller cost. Apparently there were no heart-burnings over accepted facts of this kind; the cottage maiden and her good mother did not envy the splendors of the Squire's lady and the Judge's daughter. As a wave of revolt against class despotism swept over France, and then a tempest of revolution set our colonies on the safe shore of national independence, many fine, sincere and noble things came in, but one brave, exquisite and lovely thing went out. Reverence, deference, recognition of the rights and privileges of courtesy have been suffered to become almost obsolete in many quarters. It behooves us in these days to ask why, and once more to plant in our municipalities and our rural demesnes the blooming herb of reverence.

We may begin by teaching the children to behave with politeness to their elders. I have heard my kinswomen of a former generation tell how they stood in the presence of their fathers and mothers, unless they were requested to sit. Mrs. Sherwood and Frederika Bremer describe in their autobiographies a similar custom in their childish days. With the swing of the pendulum which has reversed so much of the old order, has, unfortunately, resulted a state of affairs in which, so to speak, parents stand and children sit. In far too many households, not in the least for their own happiness and well being, children are autocrats and arbiters, and do as they please in most of their relations to home and social life. Barbara and Timothy attend a Sabbath-school which does not belong to the parental church, and they go to church or stay away as they choose. Miriam calmly swings her little feet from the most luxurious chair in the room, while grandpapa contents himself with anything he can find. Jacky plays soldier in the halls and tears madly up and down stairs, whooping like an Indian brave, while his mother struggles heroically with a nervous headache, but does not interfere with the boy, lest he shall not be happy in his home. The juvenile contingent owns the place, and, by a method of natural induction, learns that it is not worth while to show much attention to any one not of its especial world.

Yet, whoever so trains or so mistrains a child that he or she reaches maturity without the spirit and the practice of deference to authority and consideration to others, does that child a most grievous wrong. No other charm of girlhood is so winsome, no attraction of youthful manhood so potential as that habit of courtesy which has its root in an acknowledgment of the claims of infirmity, of weakness, of superior age and of honorable station. The truly well-bred person does not appear crude and ill-mannered, or arrogant and self-assertive in the presence of those whom he has the grace to treat with respect.

The quaint, sweet word decorum is not lacking in fragrance; it perfumes, as with lavender from an old-time garden, the intercourse of society where reverence is still known and practiced.

A deep courtesy and a profound bow are, each in its place, more elegant than the curt nod which is far too common. The hat taken off the head, not merely touched or lifted, is a sign of fine breeding, more common among gentlemen of the courtly old school than among hurried men of the new. Even the disuse of the beautiful term "lady," and the substitution in season and out of season, of the word "woman," are significant of an epoch when manners are degenerate, and brusqueness is exalted above the sweet refinements of delicate ceremony.

Every boy in the land should be drilled scrupulously by his mother in the accomplishment of lifting his hat or pulling off his cap when he says "good morning" or "good evening" to people whom he meets. The lad should learn to stand bareheaded when talking to an older friend, certainly to a woman on the street, unless the inclemency of the weather affords him an excuse for covering in her presence. Children on their way to school along country roads should be taught to acknowledge, with a pleasant bow, the presence of the people whom they pass. But these are merely externals of ordinary politeness which should never have been allowed to drop into desuetude. The true spirit of reverence ought to go deeper. Witness how often and how rudely children and young people interrupt their elders, how their concerns take precedence of every other interest, how they clamor for their way, and how easily they get it. I have seen a young and beautiful girl, the graduate of a famous college, lead the conversation in a drawing-room where were seated a group of people, several of whom were entitled to be called personages. That one had gained honors in the Civil War, that another was an eminent professional man, that two or three ladies were leaders in the benevolences of the city and State made no impression whatever on the young woman, who simply chattered away, monopolizing the floor, herself her heroine.

I know a girl who is plain as to feature and awkward as to form, whose opportunities have been few, and whose culture is narrow, yet she never goes anywhere or stays under any roof that her influence is not felt, as gentle as the south wind, as perfumed as the violets breath. Her secret is simplicity and deference. She forgets herself. She puts others first. The elderly lady, the old gentleman, in her code are entitled to deference when they speak, and to the best seats by the hearth and at the board. She is beloved, because she gives much and requests little.

I wish we might all pay more attention to our manners. Manner is the concrete expression of one's nature and character; it is partly inherited; it is developed from within rather than acquired from without; but manners are the product of habits. They may be taught, they may be learned, they are somewhat affected by association, and they derive a great deal from imitation. No child should sit still when a lady, his mother or his aunt, or a friend of the family, enters the room. The child should rise and remain standing till the lady is seated. The same courtesy should be shown a gentleman with the dignity of years upon his head. No young man or woman should monopolize conversation or rudely contradict the expressions of an older person. Indeed rudeness is a quality to be ruled out of human intercourse as soon as possible.

But we may rise to a higher plane. Dr. Holmes habitually went to church that he might cultivate the plant of reverence in his soul. How is it with men, old, young and of middle age, who by scores and hundreds are absent from their pews every Sabbath, excusing themselves on this and the other plea of weariness or indifference, and letting wives and daughters and sisters worship alone? They lounge at home, reading secular books and newspapers, treating the house of God as though it were a useless interruption of a man's routine, and flinging defiance in the face of the Almighty, who has said, "Ye shall keep my Sabbaths and reverence my sanctuaries."[1] What reverence for God's word is inculcated in homes where there is no family prayer, or for God's providential oversight at tables where no blessing is asked or thanks rendered? How shall a household learn to revere the Lord, when evidently money and fashion and ambition and display and pleasure are objects of worship rather than the Heavenly Father?

All foolish jesting which makes light of religion, all sneering at piety, all taking of God's name and attributes in vain, militate against reverence in character. I cannot protest too strongly against any use of the Bible which is not thoughtful and devotional. To take the words of scripture to cap a pun or

1 Leviticus 26:2.

solve a conundrum seems to me blasphemous.

Another point on which we may profitably dwell is demeanor in God's house. When the church is made a place where friends whisper and talk before service, where they carry on bits of chat at intervals during its progress, where they look over hymn-books or the church programs during a sermon that tires them, or stare about during a prayer, good manners are violated, and reverence is hopelessly at fault. Persons who assume their outdoor wraps during doxology or benediction are anything but reverential; those who shut their psalters and hymn-books with emphasis and dash them back into the rack with the rattle of musketry, manifest ignorance of propriety, and those who rush from a church the instant of dismissal, as if fleeing from a pestilence, are equally wanting in the elements of good behavior. Reverence for God's house is as essential a matter of right Christian conduct as reverence for God's word. Let none lay a profane finger on the ark of the Lord.

In our closets, too, we may cultivate reverence. Let us reflect on the way we pray. How often do we hurry into the Divine presence, hasten through our selfish catalogue, and say "Amen" with a sense of relief. I can remember my father sitting for five minutes with the Book in his hand, "composing his mind," before beginning family worship, and I cannot think that in his private devotions he ever fell into unseemly haste.

We have caught the temper of the period—a temper of unrest, of fever, of frantic endeavor to be first, and to get on. Automobiles run over little children and infirm old people, crushing them under their Juggernaut wheels; trains wait for no man's leisure; electricity belts the globe—yet still the stars keep on their everlasting courses and the God of nature holds the winds in his fist, and in the heaven above us abides the serenity of eternity, where time shall be no more.

When we stand before the great white throne, when we bow at Jesus' feet, shall we not be reverent then? O friends, let us be reverent now. In wonder, and adoration, and awe let us praise the King, whose constant care is over us, whose everlasting arms are beneath us, whose love is our dwelling place. Let us be reverent in the presence of our Father in heaven.

Browning, in one of his most excellent lyrics, speaks of commencing every day's work with "bent head and beseeching hands"[1] that so upon it might descend the blessing from above. Is there not here for our every common day and little task an example by which we might profit?

1 A quote from *The Ring and the Book* by Robert Browning.